T0209233

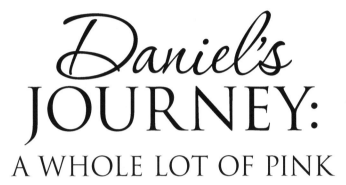

Daniel's JOURNEY:
A WHOLE LOT OF PINK

A Testimony of Faith, Hope, and Determination

MEREDITH LOCKLAR-HATCHER

WESTBOW
PRESS®
A DIVISION OF THOMAS NELSON
& ZONDERVAN

WestBow Press books may be ordered through booksellers or by contacting:

WestBow Press
A Division of Thomas Nelson & Zondervan
1663 Liberty Drive
Bloomington, IN 47403
www.westbowpress.com
1 (866) 928-1240

ISBN: 978-1-5127-9089-4 (sc)
ISBN: 978-1-5127-9090-0 (hc)
ISBN: 978-1-5127-9091-7 (e)

Library of Congress Control Number: 2017909353

Print information available on the last page.

WestBow Press rev. date: 06/14/2017

Dedication

To My Daniel. Thank you for fighting. Thank you for showing determination, even when you didn't want to. Thank you for loving Addison and for loving me. Addison and I love you so dearly. You are my hero.

To My God. You ordered each step. You put each person in the right place. You guarded and mended our hearts. You gave us hope. You are my everything.

Acknowledgments

To some of the unsung heroes during Daniel's journey: my sisters, Julianne, Whitney, and Cameron. Without you, I would not have had clean clothes, medicine, phone chargers, some of the time with Addison, and my sanity. Thank you for visiting daily and loving me constantly. I love you to the moon.

To my parents. You both carried me through several weeks of emotional misery. Thank you for just being there. You came every day and loved Daniel as your own child. I love you *this* much.

To Daniel's family. Thank you for including me in your life and treating me as family. Thank you for loving Addison as your own. You are all so incredibly special. Even Andy, who makes picture frames crooked to drive me crazy.

To our prayer warriors. Thank you is simply insufficient for what we owe you. You have been following our love story and Daniel's journey through this trial from the very beginning. Thank you for calling out to God on our behalf. Your encouragement and prayers are priceless.

To my "Uncle Boss," Joel, and Aunt Teri. Thank you for allowing me the time I needed to help and grieve. Thank you for loving Daniel and providing a place for him to live in Troy. I love you both!

To April. God gave me a solid rock as a best friend the day He let you sit by me in class at Troy State University. You put me in this position, you know, the day you set me up to meet Daniel. And I adore you for it.

Daniel's Journey

It was just another normal day … Doesn't every tragedy start off that way? This one is no different. The difference comes in the journey, and ultimately the outcome. This story has nothing to do with what the color pink would normally make you think. This isn't about babies or breast cancer. Or is it?

Let me begin by giving you a little background. My name is Meredith. I'm a child of God, mother, daughter, sister, aunt, cousin to many, and friend to all. I have an extraordinary life that is filled with family, friends, love, and laughter on a daily basis. I have a daughter, Addison, from my previous marriage. She and I met a handsome, soft-spoken guy named Daniel through a mutual friend in May of 2014. After a few weeks of talking over the phone long distance, Daniel and I decided to go on a date. Like a true gentleman, Daniel drove an hour to my house to pick me up, and then we drove another hour to dinner and a baseball game. The rest, my friends, is history.

In September of 2015, Daniel decided that he wanted to be closer to my daughter and me, so he began looking for jobs in my hometown of Troy, Alabama. In November 2015, he was hired by a local cablevision and communications provider, and he moved to Troy. He was on a crew that worked all over Southeast Alabama, digging and installing cables and fiber-optic lines for telephone, internet, and cable television. Why is that important? Because on the job is where this journey began.

Chapter 1

On Monday, January 11, 2016, after a normal day of work, Daniel and I made snacks, put on our team colors, and hunkered down in the den to watch the Alabama Crimson Tide defeat the Clemson Tigers for the BCS National Championship. It was a long, emotionally exhausting, late night. The next morning would come all too quickly as Daniel's work day started at 5:45 a.m.

On Tuesday, January 12, 2016, while on the job at a work site in Dothan, Alabama, Daniel pinched and cut his left index finger. A few minutes later, after cleaning and bandaging the cut, Daniel passed out. He was standing on the ground when he fell straight backward, hitting the back of his head on concrete. Someone from his crew immediately dialed 911, and an ambulance was dispatched to their location. The ambulance was only a few miles away, and the accident site was less than a mile from the hospital. The crew did everything the dispatcher told them to do to keep his head still and keep him calm until the ambulance got there. Daniel was taken to the emergency department at Southeast Alabama Medical Center in Dothan. Already, we see God at work saving Daniel's life.

When Daniel applied for his job, he listed me as his emergency contact. As a result, I received a call from his employer letting me know he had cut his finger and passed out and was being checked out at the hospital. I didn't think too much about it at the time. I told my boss the circumstances and left work to drive an hour to the hospital where he was being treated because I knew he would need a ride home. Surely they wouldn't make him go back to work, right? What I didn't know was the severity of his injuries.

On the drive to the hospital, I received and made several calls. First, I called Daniel's mom, Wanda. She was at work, but I wanted her to know what was going on. I told her I would call her when I knew something more or when we headed home. I also called my parents and sisters to request prayer. A few minutes later, I called Daniel's boss, Chad, who had already gotten to the hospital. I wanted to let him know I was on my way and would be there soon. I could hear in his voice that something wasn't right. He told me to call him when I was almost there and he would come out to meet me.

When I was only a few miles away, I called Chad again. While I was on the phone with him, the neurosurgeon, Dr. Hargett, came in asking questions about the accident and Daniel's medical history. Chad put me on speaker phone with the doctor, and I gave him all the information he requested, including the telephone numbers of Daniel's next of kin. I sent my dad a two-word text, "Please come." He responded "Ok," and he was on his way. You see, I'm a daddy's girl, and I had a feeling I was going to need my daddy that day.

Within minutes, I walked into the emergency room where I was directed to a certain room number. When I rounded the corner, I saw Chad. His eyes were red, and his face was filled with concern. I looked across the room, on the other side of a curtain, and saw a man lying on a hospital bed, hooked up to a ventilator. Nurses were surrounding him. They were adjusting pumps, pushing medications through IVs, and making notes on the computer. That's when recognition hit me. That man lying there hooked up to machines was my Daniel. After a moment of stunned silence, I turned to Chad and asked what had happened. He relayed to me what information he had gotten from the job-site supervisor. Then the nurses started asking questions. *Does he drink alcohol? Does he smoke? Does he do recreational drugs? Is he on any medications? Has he had any surgeries? Is he allergic to any medication?* I answered each question the best I knew how. My legs started feeling weak, and I sat in a chair across the room from the nurses and Daniel. I just prayed. I put my head down in my hands and prayed.

Sometime later, I heard the nurse tell me that if I wanted to, I could come and hold Daniel's hand. So I did. They had been trying to get him to open his eyes and respond to them, but they were having little success. While I was sitting there staring at Daniel, I was taking in every sight. There was gauze taped around his left index finger, but there was absolutely no visible damage to indicate a serious head injury. Daniel attempted to turn his head to the side at one point, and that's when I noticed a small scrape, about the size of a quarter, on the very back of his head. It simply looked like when someone skins a knee, except it was on the back of his head, and it wasn't even bleeding.

A moment later, Dr. Hargett came in and asked me to come with him. He took me to a little room where there were computers with images of the brain and skull pulled up. He explained to me that Daniel's skull had been fractured on the left side, all the way from the back to the front, and his soft spot had reopened in the front. There was swelling and minimal bleeding on the brain, but the extent of the injuries would be unknown for a few days. He also explained that the sedation and ventilator were precautionary due to Daniel's combative nature upon admission. He had to be sedated and kept still in order to get accurate scans of his head. While this reassured me that he could breathe on his own if he needed to, it did nothing for the aching in my heart and the feeling of helplessness.

Dr. Hargett asked if I had any questions, and then he walked me back to Daniel's room. A short time later, my dad arrived, and Chad left to go to the job site. My dad held me, even in his own state of shock. We prayed for Daniel. My heart cried out for miracles from Heaven. I tried to keep Daniel calm as the sedation began to wear off, but after choking due to the ventilator, the sedation had to be increased again. As we sat watching monitors, watching the rise and fall of Daniel's chest, and listening to the beeps and bells of the machines, an older gentleman, the hospital chaplain, came in and asked if he could pray with us. Of course we welcomed him to pray and asked that he continue to do so over the coming days. Within the next half hour, they moved Daniel to the critical care unit, room 448.

I sat in the CCU waiting room while the nurses got Daniel settled into his new room. Approximately twenty minutes later, they called for me to come back and see Daniel. I left my dad in the waiting room and went back to talk to the nurse. Jeremy was his name. Nurse Jeremy was so gentle and kind to me. He explained the machines and medicines that were being given to Daniel. He let me stay with Daniel for a few minutes, and then, as I was returning to the waiting room to sit with my dad, Dr. Hargett pulled me aside again. He kept saying, "This is a serious injury. It's bad. If he can recover, it will take months or years, not days or weeks."

It would be another hour before Daniel's parents could get to the hospital and hear firsthand from the mouth of the doctor the critical nature of Daniel's injuries.

> **January 12—Dothan, Alabama (Original Facebook Post)**
> **Calling on my prayer warriors. My Love, Daniel, was in an accident at work today which resulted in a serious head injury. Please pray for healing. For God's will. For Strength and Wisdom.**

> **January 12—Dothan, Alabama (Facebook Update)**
> **We don't know a whole lot different about Daniel. He is completely sedated and on a ventilator so that his body and brain can rest. The most recent scans are about the same as the first, which is a good sign for now. Not getting worse. They will repeat the neurological assessments throughout the night and the CT and CTV scans around 6am. Until then, we pray. And pray. And pray. And pray.**

I was raised in a Christian home by Christian parents. My dad is also my pastor. I have three sisters who also love the Lord, and we worship together each Sunday at my dad's church. I'm a Christian—a believer in Jesus Christ. It is because of His love for this broken, undeserving, sinful human being that He died a horrible death on a wooden cross filled with splinters. He died just so that I could have a chance to know real love—agape love—and never experience an eternal death. He wants me with Him eternally in heaven. Why? I don't know. I certainly don't deserve it. But I am so thankful. And I know these things, but I was screaming in my heart, *Why, God? I know You are with us. So why would You let this happen?* A verse that I have known since childhood would sneak into my thoughts at times. "Trust in the Lord with all your heart and lean not on your own understanding" (Proverbs 3:5 NIV). Little bits of peace came from that verse. I certainly didn't understand anything that was happening at the moment.

I did, however, understand that it is because of this great love, this eternal relationship that I have with Jesus Christ, that I was able to stand by Daniel's side and be his advocate with the physicians and nurses during this unknown journey. I struggled. Don't get me wrong. I had my Doubting Thomas moments when I felt alone and abandoned. A wise friend once said these words to me: "While the future is so unclear to me and I cannot understand anything, He is already there waiting for me in a place of peace and understanding on the other side of my hurt. I will be okay." The future and the outcome of this life's trials are complete mysteries to me. But it's like God was tapping me on the shoulder and saying, *Turn to Me. I'm right here.*

Beeps, tones, pumps, tubes, needles, suction, gauze, iodine ... If I hear and smell those familiar things again, it will be entirely too soon. Day one of this journey ended with friends and family driving in, crying with us, talking to and praying with us, and attempting to sleep in the hallway outside of the locked CCU doors. Late that night, my dad returned home.

Chapter 2

Mannitol, Keppra, Diprivan, IV Tylenol, Sodium … I have learned more about certain medications, chemicals, and life-saving measures than I ever imagined I would need to know. Who knew that ventilators had heated coils? I certainly didn't.

I was braced for impact as his parents and I entered Daniel's CCU room the next morning. To our surprise, Daniel had been extubated and was breathing on his own. However, he wasn't overly responsive. He had his eyes tightly shut, and his forehead was wrinkled with tension. He wouldn't open his eyes or really follow commands. At the time, the nurses told us that his lack of responsiveness was because he was still coming out of the sedation. I wasn't overly comforted with the reasoning because I know just enough about Diprivan to know that it leaves the system fairly quickly. Regardless, we were so happy to see his unobstructed face. His color was great. His vitals were strong. He was just unresponsive. Knowing that his body had experienced great trauma, we chose not to get too upset and to just let him rest. We left the room thanking God for his protection over Daniel and praying for his nurses.

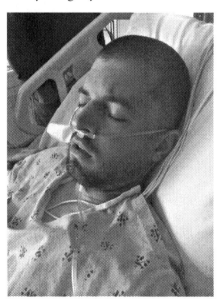

Daniel

January 13—Dothan, Alabama (Facebook Update)
    We just came out from seeing Daniel. He is off the ventilator and they are weaning the meds so that he will wake up. He is in quite some pain which is obvious by his facial expressions. His vitals are ok and his repeat CT and CTV scans this morning showed no worsening of the swelling or bleeding. At this point there is no surgery in the plan. But friends, prayer warriors, he has a LONG road of recovery ahead of him assuming the next 48 hours remain stable. This is a very serious head and brain trauma. We thank you for, and still covet your prayers!!! God is so good!!!

One of the hardest things about having a loved one in the CCU is the strict policy on visiting hours. Being able to see the love of your life for only thirty minutes four times a day just wasn't going to cut it for me. My Daniel needed me. I needed him. I prayed really hard about this need, and once again, God answered favorably. For the most part, if we were quiet and did not interrupt the nurse's need to do hourly neurological checks on Daniel, we were allowed to stay a little longer than the designated thirty minutes. Out of respect for the nurses and doctors, we tried not to wear out our welcome, but we did take advantage of the extra time with Daniel.

January 13—Dothan, Alabama (Facebook Update)
    We saw Daniel again. He is opening his eyes a little more often but not keeping them open. He isn't communicating verbally at all yet but its still really early to expect that kind of progress. He is still off the ventilator, vitals look good, and he is stable. We will see him again at 4:30. Please, please, please pray fervently for Daniel!!!

It was at this point in this journey that I began really grilling the doctors and nurses and advocating for Daniel. I needed to know the reason for every medication, every finger prick, and every IV pump. I quickly became known as "the girlfriend" to some, and "the fiancé" to others.

Some even thought that Daniel and I were already married. It made me a happy girl to know that his parents included my telephone number on Daniel's chart as a person to contact in case of emergency. Little did we know that my phone number would be vital in the very near future. We didn't realize it then, but God was already preparing us for a storm.

> **January 13—Dothan, Alabama (Facebook Update)**
> **Thankful for the little things right now. Just saw Daniel. Got to spend an hour with him. His vitals are still stable and he still isn't opening his eyes much. He still hasn't tried to talk but we pray those things come with time. Physical Therapy came and sat him up on the side of the bed. They tried to help him stand but obviously he couldn't yet. Those things will come. I know they will. My God is SO good and in control!!!**

At the last visiting hour for the evening, Daniel's vitals remained strong, however, his responses were somewhat slower. We didn't push him to do what we asked, but rather we talked to him and encouraged him to fight. I prayed over Daniel, and then we left the room.

After that visiting hour was over, one of my sisters and her husband stopped by to check on us. My brother-in-law asked if he could see Daniel. I called the night nurse, Autumn, from the hallway telephone and she allowed me to take him back to see Daniel for a short time. My brother-in-law was in shock to see Daniel in his current condition. I told Daniel that we were in the room, but got no response. I asked Daniel to squeeze my hand, but got no response. In the fifteen minutes between when his parents and I were visiting, until I returned with my brother-in-law, Daniel's responses were drastically different. When we left the room, I was crying. Nurse Autumn came to talk to me. I told her about Daniel's lack of response and she promised to go in right away and do a thorough neurological exam. She hugged me, and then my brother-in-law and I left to return to the waiting room.

One of the biggest and most important parts of caring for someone who is ill or injured is to know Who is ultimately in control. Without a doubt, God is ultimately in control. It was important to me to know that the doctors and nurses caring for Daniel believed in God and were willing to pray about their decisions regarding Daniel's care. Each new face I saw in Daniel's room got asked the same question, "Do you believe in God and the power of prayer?" Nurse Autumn promised to take good care of Daniel. She would be an answer to prayer and vital part of Daniel's care.

God had already showed up and started showing out by placing people in our path to remind us that He was with us. One of those people was a godly lady who has known me my entire life and who works at that hospital. Her name is Kelli. Kelli proved to be a huge source of strength and humor while we were at the hospital. Even her daughters were very generous and offered to run errands and do laundry for me while I was at the hospital. After two days in the hospital, Kelli insisted that I come to her house and get a good night of sleep. She reminded me that I am no good to Daniel if I don't take care of myself. So that night, I went to Kelli's house, got a shower, and got ready for bed.

As I started to lie down, I cried uncontrollably. Every night for the time Daniel and I had been dating, I had called him before I went to sleep. That night, in the quiet of that room, I realized I couldn't call him. I couldn't tell him good night. I was a mess. In recent years, I have suffered from extreme anxiety, especially at night, and have been prescribed medication to help me sleep. That night, I took a sleeping pill and crashed in a heavenly soft bed. Daniel's parents got a hotel room and went there to sleep.

Chapter 3

At 10:59 p.m., my cell phone rang. It was a Dothan number that I didn't recognize. I answered and was told to "hold for the doctor." Just for the record, that's never good. By this time, I was sitting up straight in the bed. Dr. Voss, another neurosurgeon in the practice with Dr. Hargett, picked up the phone. He stated that Daniel's neurological status had changed. He was unresponsive again, and they were taking him for stat computerized tomography (CT) and CT Venogram scans. If the scans showed swelling, they would take him directly to surgery. He asked if I could come back to the hospital to sign consents for surgery. I told him I would get in touch with Daniel's parents and be there as soon as possible.

I spoke to Daniel's parents, and they rushed back to the hospital. I, however, was stuck. I was in no position to drive since I had taken sleep medication. All I could do was call my mom and dad and cry. My dad got right back in his truck and drove the hour to Dothan to be with Daniel's parents. He made me stay and try to sleep and promised to keep me updated. I knew that if he thought I needed to be there, he would come get me. So I tried to sleep … without much success.

The next morning (Thursday), I got up early and drove to the hospital. My dad was still there and met me in the hallway. I guess if you have to hear hard news, it is best for it to come from someone you love. My dad told me that the surgery had gone well, but the swelling of Daniel's brain was significant. They had to remove part of his skull on the right side to allow for the swelling. Dr. Voss had told them that there would most likely be changes in Daniel as a result of the brain swelling. Daniel may have a handicap or personality changes, but the severity could not be predicted. Only time would tell. The next seventy-two hours were absolutely critical, and the only goal of the doctors was to keep Daniel alive.

There is a part of me that is ashamed to say this, but there was a moment that I prayed that if Daniel would not have an excellent quality of life after this injury and the surgery, that God would take him and not let him suffer. But God had much bigger plans than what my tiny little mind could fathom.

January 14—Dothan, Alabama (Facebook Update)
I apologize for few updates today. Here's what I know, which is very little. Last night after visiting hours Daniel's condition deteriorated pretty drastically. He was unresponsive. I received a call from the hospital telling me that they were putting him back on the ventilator, taking him for another CT, and depending on what they found, straight to surgery. While the results of the CT were not drastically different, they were enough different that they had altered Daniel's status. Daniel was taken to surgery where his right skull flap was removed to allow for swelling to occur without creating additional pressure. He is very critical. Right now we are focused on saving his life, and nothing more.

I just came out from seeing him again. His color is great. His vitals are strong. He is moving all extremities and rolling from side to side to get comfortable. He is still sedated and intubated and restrained, but I am so thankful for the little signs we are seeing: movement of his arms and legs, pupils back to being equal with a little bilateral movement, his gag reflex is intact ...

I spent time scratching and rubbing his back again, and I sang to him quietly for a few minutes. I pray over him every time I get my hands on him. I'm thankful but still greatly concerned.

PRAY. PRAY. PRAY. PRAY.

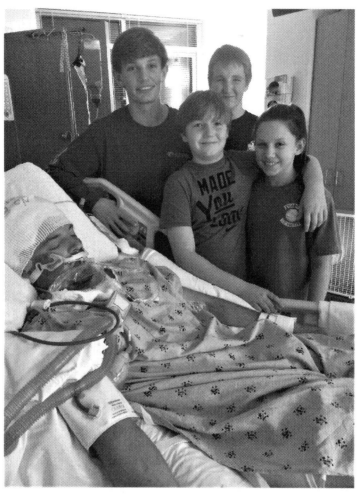

**Daniel with his nephews, Bryan, Wade,
& Daulton, and niece, Sydney.**

When I first got to see Daniel that morning, he was once again intubated. His arms were restrained, and his head was wrapped in white gauze. There was a piece of tape across the gauze that said in bold black letters, "NO RIGHT FLAP." There was a big sign on the wall at the head of his bed that said, "NO BONE FLAP ON RIGHT." What that means is that there was a piece of Daniel's skull that had been removed from the right side of his head to allow for swelling of the brain without further pressure from the skull. The skull flap had been placed in a sterile container and put in a freezer until the time came to replace it. The skin over the area had been stapled back into place to keep the site sterile. Within hours after surgery, we were seeing improvements in Daniel's responsiveness. We held on with great hope to every little movement or flutter of the eyes. What we once took for granted, we now celebrated.

More family and friends came. I thank God for my three sisters. My family was my rock. Our cell phones were ringing constantly. Between visits with Daniel, we tried to answer messages, update our statuses on Facebook so that our prayer warriors would know how to pray, and simply breathe. I am not exaggerating. At times I literally had to remind myself to stop holding my breath. I had absolutely no appetite, but that didn't stop people from trying to get me to eat. I snacked mostly, feeling that if I ate too much, I would be sick.

> **January 14—(Facebook Post by Meredith's Sister, Cameron)**
> **"Sisters" is one of the greatest bonds there is. This week has reminded me how grateful I am to be one of four. Prayer partners, support system, a shoulder to cry on, someone to laugh with (and at), and best friends. I'm not sure how people without siblings get through times like this. My sisters are the best!**

So many people who love us brought baskets of snacks; crossword, word-find and Sudoku puzzle books; coloring books and crayons; plastic bags of quarters to be used at the vending machines; and anything else we could imagine needing. A local family-owned restaurant even provided meals for our family. Financial donations were made to help us pay for meals, hotel rooms, and everyday necessities. I took some of that money and bought Daniel a radio clock for his hospital room. I needed him to be able to hear familiar music and sounds, not just scary beeping and suction noises. To say that we were blessed by everything donated is an understatement.

We continued to see God providing us with the most spectacular nurses. Nurse Lisa was affectionately named "Mama Lisa." Older and more experienced than many of her colleagues, she proved to be motherly in the way she cared for Daniel. Mama Lisa also believed in the power of prayer and spent time praying for Daniel. She talked to him just as if he were awake and listening. I specifically remember walking into the room one time and she was saying, "Baby boy, why could you have not been standing on the grass?" That warmed my heart, and it gave me such a peace while Daniel was under her watchful eye.

> **January 15—Dothan, Alabama (Facebook Update)**
> **Just saw Daniel. He opened his eyes for the first time since surgery while we were back there. The nurse said, "OH, I haven't seen that!" I told him to squeeze my hands several times and he did, all except one time. He's still active. I leaned by his ear and told him I love him and kissed his temple area. He leaned his face over towards mine and stayed there until I moved. I'm holding tight to those things. We also met with the Neuro Surgeon on call today. He was nice. A Florida Gator fan, but nice. He pinched Daniel and boy did Daniel make a face and try to twist away from him. His pupils are responsive but a little asymmetrical. I told him about Daniel responding to me and he said, "Oh yeah, he will respond." I made the doctor give me a high five.**
>
> **We are still in a very critical state. Another 24 hours will tell us a lot. Honestly, we are still just focused on saving his life. Please keep praying! Our God is SO good and He gets all the glory in this! He is able and He loves us!**

At this point, I started fading. The adrenaline was wearing off. I found myself spending more time curled up in the waiting room chairs with my blanket and pillow and sleeping away the time. I very vividly remember waking up with what I knew to be a reminder from God Himself on my heart. "Because of the Lord's great love we are not consumed, for his compassions never fail. They are new every morning; great is your faithfulness" (Lamentations 3:22–23 NIV). *Hold on, Meredith. I'm working. Remain faithful. Don't doubt me.*

No sooner than those words crossed my mind, another Bible verse did as well. "But he said to me, 'My grace is sufficient for you, for my power is made perfect in weakness.' Therefore I will boast all the more gladly about my weaknesses, so that Christ's power may rest on me" (2 Corinthians 12:9 NIV). *Be vulnerable. Love me. Others will see my power through your weakness, and certainly through Daniel's weakness right now.* "But I don't want Daniel to be weak! I want him to be strong! I need him to fight to get better! I need him to be determined to come through this and come back to me!" I felt like a toddler pitching a fit in the middle of the floor, stomping my feet. *Remember, I'm working. Don't doubt me. Watch for My hand in the small things as well as the big things.*

That afternoon, the same hospital chaplain came by to check on us. He had been in to pray with Daniel. He stopped by to see if we needed anything, and he saw the worry in my eyes. He looked directly at me and said, "Stop taking this away from our God. Give it to Him and then sit on your hands if you have to. Let Him do the work." This was a turning point for me. The Holy Spirit was stirring in my soul and reminding me that God never leaves me to figure things out on my own or carry the weight of the world by myself. He loves me, and He is everywhere! I needed those blinders to be removed so that I could see God working in Daniel's life. Since our time there, that sweet chaplain has retired. I have no doubt that God left him there just for us.

By the evening visit, Daniel's color was great, his vitals were strong, his pupils were equal and reactive, and his gag reflex was intact. He was moving his arms and legs and trying to roll from side to side. We were told that all of these were good neurological signs. One thing that concerned me was the possibility of bed sores. So each time Daniel would try to roll to the side, I would reach down behind his back and massage his shoulders and shoulder blades, or scratch his back. It quickly became apparent that he liked to have his back scratched. Humorously, I made it known to the nurses that if he rolled to the side, I expected them to scratch his back. His nurses were such great sports. That day, we held tightly to each squeeze of the hand, each wiggle of the toes, and each flutter of his eye lids.

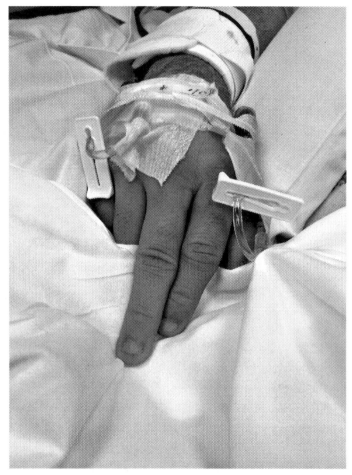

"Two Fingers, Daniel!"

January 16—Dothan, Alabama (Facebook Update)

Do you know what this means? Do you know? Daniel was asked to hold up 2 fingers ... AND HE DID!!! I wiped the sleepy out of his eyes with a wash cloth and told him to look at me ... AND HE DID!!! We asked him to wiggle his toes ... AND HE DID!!! My GOD is SO BIG, SO STRONG and SO MIGHTY! There's NOTHING my GOD cannot do!!! I finally heard the words out of a doctor's mouth, "He's stable." Out of the woods? Well, not quite. But so much closer!

His Neuro Surgeon met with us this morning too and said he is "honestly amazed" at Daniel's progress post-surgery. There is still a long road ahead, but Daniel is fighting through this! He is still getting "food" and tolerating it well. To say I'm in awe of God at this point is an understatement. Keep praying!!!

Over the next twenty-four hours, Daniel progressed so well that the neurosurgeon said he was "honestly amazed." Daniel squeezed hands on command, and opened his eyes for the first time while we were in the room with him. God granted me a glimpse of His power when He allowed Daniel to respond to my affections. Since the surgery was on his right side, I would kiss Daniel's left temple area. Less than forty-eight hours after surgery, Daniel would lean his left cheek against my face when I would kiss him. I felt like that was one of God's ways of wrapping His arms around me in a big hug!

Chapter 4

Oh, the winds of change. We were so close to reaching the seventy-two-hour post-surgery goal when Daniel's neurological responses began to decline again. I mentioned before that Nurse Autumn would play a vital role in Daniel's care. Nurse Autumn quickly made note of the changes in Daniel's neurological status and took charge. The neurosurgeon was notified, and new CT scans were done. Then, the waiting game began. We had to wait to hear from the doctor. What else could we do but pray?

By 2 a.m., we still had not heard what the most recent scans showed. Most people would assume that no news is good news. But I couldn't wait any longer without hearing anything. I called Nurse Autumn from the CCU hallway telephone. She opened the doors and let me go back to sit with Daniel for a while. I made a mental note that more medications were hanging on the IV pole, one of which was Mannitol—the medication first given to Daniel to reduce swelling of his brain. In the quiet of the 2 a.m. hour, I sat next to the bed, holding his hands, quietly singing praise and worship songs, and praying over Daniel. I rejoiced in the steadiness of his vitals and thanked God for the apparent rest Daniel was getting. After some time, I have no idea how long, I thanked Nurse Autumn and returned to the waiting room. I sat up the rest of the night, journaling and praying.

At the first regularly scheduled visiting hour, Daniel was somewhat more responsive. His eyes were still closed most of the time, but he did respond to us and open them on command more often. He did squeeze our hands and hold up two fingers when told to do so. We all breathed a sigh of relief.

It was an unspoken understanding between Daniel's parents and myself that at least one of us would always be at the hospital with Daniel, either in his room or in the waiting room. We took turns going to the hotel to shower, leaving to go to the store, or simply going downstairs to the cafeteria. At least one of us was always accessible to Daniel or by the doctor.

After the first morning visit was over, I went across the street to the hotel and took a shower. Having not slept the night before, I set my alarm on my phone and decided to rest for one hour. Then, no sooner than I pulled the covers over me, my phone rang. Daniel's dad called to say that Dr. Voss, the neurosurgeon who had performed Daniel's surgery, had come by to tell them that the scans from the night before showed that Daniel's brain was "full." If they did not do surgery to remove the left side bone flap, the pressure from the swelling would kill him. With wet hair and no makeup, I threw my stuff in my car and rushed back across the street to the hospital.

When I was pulling into the parking lot, I noticed a familiar car. My best friend, April, and her family, had decided to come be with us on this particular Sunday. God knew I needed her. He sent her to hug me and hold me. I jumped out of my car, yelled across the parking lot that he was being taken into emergency surgery, and then ran to the CCU. Breathlessly, I sent a voice text to my three sisters, knowing they were in church. I needed them to pray. My older sister, Julianne, interrupted the sermon, and the whole church stopped to pray for Daniel. I have chill bumps from head to toe thinking about the love and response of my church. How do people without a church family make it through the toughest of times without losing their sanity?

As soon as I arrived at the CCU waiting room, I dropped my bag and ran to the CCU doors, called the nurses' station, and was let back to see Daniel before they took him to surgery. To be honest, I was not happy. Okay, I was furious. I started questioning everything. Why are we just now doing surgery, fifteen hours after the scan was performed? Why were we not told sooner about the results of the scan? What exactly is the plan? Is Daniel strong enough to withstand another surgery like this? I wanted to hold someone responsible for the delayed surgery. I was one mad girlfriend.

I talked to Daniel, and he even responded by squeezing my hand. I prayed over Daniel. When the surgery team came in to take him down, I made them stop and have prayer with us too. Nobody was getting out of that room without having been prayed over! Eventually, the nurse told me that she felt it was the doctor's plan to use the Mannitol to decrease the swelling prior to doing additional surgery. Having noticed the Mannitol drip the night before, it made sense. But I was still not happy with her explanation. As they started to wheel his bed toward the door, one of the nurses said, "Daniel, tell them bye." I said, "No! Wave to me and tell me, 'See you later!'" Then, as if God was hugging me once again, Daniel looked straight toward the door where I was standing, raised his right hand, and waved.

>Ecclesiastes 8:3–7, NIV, says:
>
>Do not be in a hurry to leave the king's presence. Do not stand up for a bad cause, for he will do whatever he pleases. Since a king's word is supreme, who can say to him, 'What are you doing?' Whoever obeys his command will come to no harm, and the wise heart will know the proper time and procedure. For there is a proper time and procedure for every matter, though a man's misery weighs heavily upon him. Since no man knows the future, who can tell him what is to come?

Jesus. Jesus reigns as King. His word is supreme, and He knows what He is doing. He was guiding, and the doctors were being led to the proper procedures, in the proper timing. I had to sit back, breathe, and remember God's promises. Daniel was in His hands.

January 17—Dothan, Alabama (Facebook Update)
Prayer Warriors! Daniel has been taken back to surgery to relieve pressure from the left side of his brain. He may have also suffered a stroke at the base of his brain. We know that GOD is in control of this situation. He is in control of Daniel's health. PRAY NOW!

The next several hours were a blur. The waiting room was packed full of Daniel's prayer warriors. Friends and Daniel's coworkers came to sit with and love on us. Some brought buckets of bottled water and Diet Mountain Dew (my favorite). Another brought me a box of Advocare Spark (an absolute necessity for me). Others showed up with more quarters for the vending machines, puzzle books, and snacks. Every time I turned around, someone was trying to make me eat. All I wanted to do was fall asleep and then wake up from this nightmare.

Eventually we received a call from surgery telling us that everything had gone well; Daniel was stable; and the doctor was closing. When Dr. Voss came to talk to us, he said he was glad he had done the surgery. Daniel's brain was indeed full, and if it had swelled any more, it would have caused major damage, possibly even death. He also confirmed that Daniel had suffered a stroke in the left occipital region of his brain, which could affect his vision. We would not know the extent of the damage until Daniel was able to talk to us coherently. I reminded him that he had asked us to give him seventy-two hours after the first surgery for Daniel to be considered "out of the woods." He then asked us for another seventy-two hours. He once again reiterated that his only objective at the moment was to keep Daniel alive.

January 17—Dothan, Alabama (Facebook Update)

Daniel is out of surgery and back in CCU. The surgery went as expected. The surgeon said he's glad he went ahead and did the surgery because the swelling had the brain "full" and any more swelling would have caused pressure and permanent damage. He now has no brain flap on either side. The next 72 hours after surgery, again, are critical. His vitals are strong and stable. He is already responding to commands. He squeezed my hand and held a tight grip for a long time. He has already pulled his legs up in the bed and rested his knees to the sides. He is in critical condition and not out of danger. Please pray for Daniel. Pray for his nurses because a patient with no brain flap on either side is not something they have experienced. His care is crucial and very sensitive at this point. Get on your knees, in your prayer closet, wherever you need to be to get closest to God, and get busy, Prayer Warriors! God has proven Himself able and He is still in the miracle business!!!

Chapter 5

It is safe to say that after taking in the report from the second surgery, I was numb. I had been told that this man whom I loved more than words would most likely have a handicap, could be blind, or may even die. I felt like my emotions were at their limit. I was about to explode with frustration! I wanted to scream at God and anyone else who would listen. For a while, I pretty much withdrew from the crowd, looking for a quiet place to scream internally. The tears were definitely external. I couldn't stop them from streaming down my face. I'm an ugly crier, but there was no way I could stop the tears.

"Really, God? I can't handle this right now. I have a daughter at home who needs me too. I am not emotionally stable enough to be what Daniel needs right now."

Be still … My grace is sufficient. I haven't asked you to carry any load that I am not prepared to help you carry.

Sometimes I wish God didn't think I was so strong. But He never fails to give me a gentle reminder that He Is. He is everything I need Him to be, when I need Him, and where I need Him. He has never failed me, and He will not start now. We often hear people say that God will not put more on us than we can handle. That's a lie. But He did promise that when we carry a heavy load, He will be there to help us carry it. We do not have to carry it alone.

When we finally got to see Daniel, his head was bandaged. There had been another big sign added to the wall above his head that said, "NO BONE FLAP ON LEFT SIDE." A nurse was at Daniel's bedside while we visited. Dr. Voss told us that the next day the bandages would be removed. Wait, what? We had not seen Daniel's head uncovered since before the first surgery. We couldn't imagine what we would see. We could tell that it took the nurse by surprise too. She, like us, thought it to be really soon to remove the bandages after the second surgery. I must admit that her shocked look was not comforting to the family. But we all agreed that God would prepare us and protect Daniel.

After the 4:30 p.m. visiting hour was over I went to the waiting room, grabbed my blanket, got on my knees in the corner of the room, pulled the blanket over my head, and prayed. "God, please prepare us for what we might see when they remove the bandages. God, please be with Daniel and heal him completely." Never once did I doubt God's presence. I knew He was hearing me. I knew He was hearing the cries of all of our prayer warriors. In a strange way, I knew He was growing me for His purpose. I had no idea why He chose this path. And I had no choice but to walk it. But I remember a time in my youth when I heard a sermon about praising God. I remember being told that there would be times when I would be praising God and crying at the same time. This was one of those times.

By the last visit, Nurse Autumn was back by Daniel's side for the night. This was an answer to prayer. Autumn was scheduled to be off so that she could pack to go out of town for ten days. She took on an extra shift before her vacation just to care for Daniel after surgery. We had grown to truly love her, and we are still very thankful for Nurse Autumn. She took good care of him that night. He was more responsive, and his vitals were strong. Before we bedded down for the night in the waiting room, Daniel's parents and I spent time praying; talking to him; exercising his hands, arms, and legs; and just loving on him. God granted me a great peace that night. I believe we all slept a little easier knowing that Nurse Autumn was on night watch.

January 17—Dothan, Alabama (Facebook Update)

Tonight when the visiting hour came around, I went back to see Daniel. As I walked down the hallway I noticed someone with long, light red hair sitting at the nurses station with her back to me. That's when it hit me. Nurse Autumn is back for the night!!! I grabbed her and hugged her and cried happy tears! God knew I needed her tonight. Once again, The Lord has provided!

Now for the most important patient. Daniel was active and responsive tonight. He followed commands

and opened his eyes. He flattered his nephews by moving his feet when they told him to. Over all, his vitals are good, his drains are good, his sodium level is good. He does have a low temp, but as before, it isn't uncommon after surgery. I spent some time with him after everyone left the room. I sang. He squeezed my hand the whole time. I told him I was going to sit and rest a while but I would be back … and he nodded his head! Now … we have the best nurse, a responsive patient, and more prayers than we deserve!

Please pray that Daniel will have a restful night of healing. Pray that Autumn will be on top of his care, alert and on point tonight. Pray that if the brain has anymore swelling to do that it is minimal and can be done without further damage. Pray that his vitals remain strong. WE WILL GIVE GOD ALL THE GLORY NOW AND ALWAYS!!! 42 more critical hours…

January 18—Dothan, Alabama (Facebook Update— early morning hours)

I just spent the last 35 minutes with the most handsome man. I needed this quiet time with him. We prayed. I sang softly. I just stood by his side and held his hand. His vitals look strong tonight. When I walked in his nurse told him he had a visitor. He looked straight at me and waved with his right hand. When I took that hand he squeezed 3 times – I believe that is his way of saying I Love You, and I'll take it.

God, I don't know why I'm so amazed. You never fail us. You are Love and Love never fails! You are healing beyond what the doctors are capable of doing. Thank You for using those doctors and nurses as your hands and tools to care for My Daniel! YOU get all the glory! I will praise YOU loud and forever!!! Please keep showing out through Daniel's care and his healing process!

Chapter 6

Have you ever prayed for poop? I have. Daniel had not eaten anything or pooped in six days. The doctor ordered feeding by tube to give Daniel some nutrition and hopefully get his bowels working. The last thing we needed was for Daniel to get constipated too. So yes, I prayed for poop.

January 18—Dothan, Alabama (Facebook Update)
Daniel is doing fairly well this morning. He is still following commands and responding the best way he knows how. His vitals are strong and steady. He is so strong. I admire his determination. He's my hero.

A few specific prayer requests:
His nurse today is the same nurse who was with him yesterday during the day when he went to surgery. She is confident in her care for Daniel, but she did say that it is "tricky." Daniel is active and likes to move his head around from side to side – which isn't exactly what we want right now.

They will be removing bandages today from Daniel's head. Please pray that those of us who love him so will be accepting of what we see and strong for Daniel's sake. We just don't know what to expect.

I know this may be TMI but they are now wanting Daniel's gut to wake up. They are "feeding" him and need his bowels to respond. Urine output is still great. We just need him to poop. So please pray in that regard as well.

Pray for continued healing and rest for Daniel's body. I thank God and praise Him for what He has accomplished through this trial in Daniel's life. Keep those prayers lifted!!!

We had a meeting with a neuropsychologist. Talk about information overload. Dr. Passler was very approachable and reassuring. He spoke to us about strokes and how certain areas of the brain that are affected by stroke or trauma can sometimes reroute themselves and compensate for lost function. The brain is so mysterious yet so fascinating. He also spoke to us about the way he measures cognitive function. It was a little disheartening to hear that Daniel had been only one point above a coma, but it was encouraging to know that he was progressing positively each day. He gave us some ideas about what to expect in the weeks and months to come as Daniel healed. He told us that Daniel would have his ups and downs, his good days and bad. There was so much that we didn't know. That's why we held on to Who we knew instead.

When we next got to see Daniel, his responses to commands were not as quick, which made me extremely nervous. I spent time praying over Daniel, as I did every single visit with him. I prayed, begging God to show up and show out. "God, please don't let him regress." I sang quietly to Daniel, exercised his arms and legs, massaged his fingers, and just tried to let him know I was there for him. Toward the end of the visit, Daniel actually gripped my hand and started rubbing his thumb around my hand. That was something he had done our whole relationship when we held hands. That simple caress assured me that my Daniel was still in there, and he was responding to me.

When the visitation time ended, I wanted to find a quiet place and pray. Thankfully, the waiting room had somewhat cleared out for a while, and it was quiet. "God, please send us a night nurse who loves You and who is good with neuro patients. God, we need You!" If I had ever doubted God's presence with us during this trial, He was about to prove Himself to me.

Janaury 18—Dothan, Alabama (Facebook Update)
Your prayers for Daniel are needed tonight. We still have 22 hours of absolutely critical time post-surgery.

Daniel still isn't really responding to commands. He is moving fine, but not doing what is asked of him. It could be a result of swelling of the brain. It could be that he is exhausted. We have no way of knowing at this moment. They have another CT scheduled for early morning prior to the doctors' rounds. They removed one of his drains, the only one left from the first surgery, and his 2 drains from the second surgery are draining well. I'm not sure who his nurse will be for tonight. Please pray that it is someone who loves The Lord and will love my Daniel. Pray for whomever to be alert and very good with neuro patients. Our God is so good! He will not fail!!!

At the last visiting hour, we were all a little anxious about seeing Daniel's head uncovered. When we rounded the corner, we saw the bandages had been removed. Thankfully, the night nurse, Kris, had placed a washcloth over Daniel's head. Nurse Kris was in the process of cleaning the iodine and blood off of Daniel's head and face. He started to rub Daniel's scalp with the cloth, and we all cringed! Daniel's mom asked him to wait until we were out of the room to clean him up because it was more than any of us could handle. For heaven's sake, Daniel didn't have a skull in two places and he was scrubbing his head like nothing was wrong! I believe it was then that God said, *I'm doing what you asked. Trust in me.*

Nurse Kris started talking to us and comforting us. He said, "Daniel has great doctors, but there is only one Great Physician." Before I knew what I was doing, I was hugging Nurse Kris. It turns out that he used to work for our neurosurgeon before he started working in the CCU. He was very familiar with all of the physicians in the Neuro Spine group, and it was his goal to one day become a neurosurgeon himself. Nurse Kris was a very specific answer to my very specific prayers. Only God could have lined up Daniel's care with such intimate perfection. That night, after visiting hours were over, I broke down into uncontrollable tears of joy and thankfulness.

January 18—Dothan, Alabama (Facebook Update)

My prayer earlier was that God would provide a nurse for Daniel tonight who loves The Lord and is great with neuro patients. Well, Prayer Warriors, He did just that!!! His name is Kris. When I walked in and introduced myself he was reassuring as to the care Daniel is getting. He said, "he has great doctors, but there is only One Great Physician!" I walked around the bed and hugged him! And guess what … He is one of our neuro surgeon's former nurses! So he knows our surgeon, he knows Daniel's needs, and he has such a positive energy about him that made us feel so good! Thank you, God, for Kris!

Daniel did respond to some commands at his 7pm neuro check. He hasn't responded a whole lot since then but he does localize pain, which is good. His vitals are still good, and his gag reflex is strong. He's still moving his legs a good bit too.

Prayer requests for tonight: That the swelling on Daniel's brain be finished swelling and start decreasing. That Kris be alert and on point with his care for Daniel tonight. That Daniel get much needed rest for his brain, his body, and his spirit. That Daniel would be encouraged and remain determined to fight to get well and for a peace and patience to face each new day.

January 19—Dothan, Alabama (Facebook Update)

Just came out from seeing Daniel. He is so very handsome. Our night nurse, Kris, took time to clean up the scalp and shave Daniel's week old beard. The swelling in his left eye is significantly less. He is responding to commands again and his vitals continue to be strong. OT came in and worked with his arms and hands. He pushed with his hand when told to. Also, the pulmonary specialist came by and talked to Daniel. He was able to shake his head in response to the doctor's questions. The doctors turned off his ventilator for a minute and he breathed ok on his own. Pulmonary is just waiting for Neuro to approve the weaning process. Also, they will be fitting him for a protective helmet today. Please continue to pray for Daniel. Pray for his day nurse, Brandie. Pray for continued decrease in swelling of his brain. Thank you for your willingness to pray! Keep them coming!!!

Chapter 7

In the days to come, occupational therapists, speech therapists, physical therapists, and pulmonary specialists would work with Daniel several times each day. His CCU room seemed to have a revolving door. Between hourly neurological checks, beeping pumps that had to be checked, and visiting hours, the chances for Daniel to truly rest seemed slim. But every bit of that constant interruption was necessary. God was ordering each step, each day.

Some things that seem scary can also be a blessing in disguise. We rejoiced in the responses we got from Daniel. It seemed, though, that the more he tried to wake up and respond to us, the more he coughed. Can you imagine having to cough with a big tube in your mouth and down your throat? Being on the ventilator made coughing scary. It was obvious that Daniel was uncomfortable when he coughed. The nurses would hurry into his room and suction the tubes to help clear his airway so that he could relax. This almost always made him gag. While gagging in itself is disturbing, having a functioning gag reflex is a good neurological sign, so we were happy to see him gag. How demented does that sound?

Positive progress meant new challenges too. Knowing that God continued to work behind the scenes was the only thing of which I could be sure. Everything else in Daniel's future, and my future with Daniel, was unknown. I was always nervous walking down the hallway to Daniel's room. I was so afraid that something would be terribly wrong when I rounded the corner and walked through his door. Then there are those times when you get great surprises. I very vividly remember turning the corner into Daniel's room and seeing his eyes open, watching the television. Basketball. The television was on the ESPN channel, and Daniel was watching basketball. If you know my Daniel, you know that basketball is his favorite sport. He was a basketball star in his own right in high school. So to see that familiar look in his eye as he followed the sounds of the television with his eyes to see what was happening was so encouraging.

We spent many days fighting a fever. Daniel was very restless at times, kicking the covers off and bending his legs up in the bed when his fever was higher. The nurses had to keep a box fan on high, blowing directly on Daniel, to help manage his fever. Because of his injury and the resulting stroke, the medications Daniel could be given to manage his fever were limited to Tylenol by IV. Blood was drawn daily to check his sugar and sodium levels, but even more was drawn for cultures to test for viral and bacterial infections. As you may know, cultures take days, not hours, to grow. Before the cultures had all the time needed to complete the growth process, Daniel's fever broke. This was one more way that God showed up in an obvious way.

Four days after the second surgery, the pulmonary specialist started weaning Daniel off of the ventilator. Thankfully, Daniel was able to tolerate the weaning process fairly well. While Daniel's ability to breathe on his own was at the top of our prayer list, we still had not stopped praying for poop. Nurse Brandie, a happy, positive, energetic nurse whom we grew to love, finally resorted to a suppository in an effort to make Daniel's bowels respond.

This particular day, Daniel was very responsive. He was keeping his eyes open longer, following the sounds of voices with his eyes, nodding or shaking his head in response to questions, and even shook my dad's hand. Suddenly, Daniel's heart rate increased to 103 beats per minute and his face turned red. Initially, I was very alarmed. I started trying to determine what was hurting and finally got a nod of his head: his stomach was hurting. Praise the Lord, he needed to poop. We all left the room to give him some privacy, and I sent in his nurse.

Chapter 8

I mentioned before about all of the gifts we received while at the hospital. All of the gifts were equally important and appreciated. There is one, however, that stood out as a means of comfort. Daniel was sent a prayer blanket from his brother's church. We spread the blanket out over Daniel, pulled a corner up to his forehead and face, and prayed all over again for healing that can only come from God. That prayer blanket stayed in Daniel's hospital and rehabilitation rooms throughout the entire journey. He would later receive another handmade prayer blanket from the church of one of his friends. That blanket too would remain in the room with Daniel throughout his rehabilitation months.

January 20 · Dothan · 🧑‍🤝‍🧑

Tonight for the first time he intertwined his fingers with mine when holding my hand. 😍

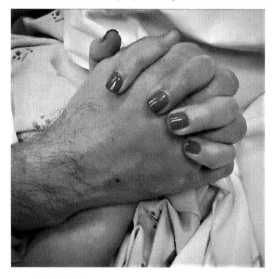

Daniel's home community in Greenville, Alabama, truly rallied around his family during this trial. Many provided gifts. Many prayed. Many watched over the house. Many helped look after Daniel's elderly grandparents. The local newspaper wrote several articles on Daniel's injury. They mentioned the impact Daniel had on the community, which is why he was so loved and supported by the whole town. I never knew my Daniel was loved by so many people. He not only had an impact on the little children whom he coached in basketball, but also on their families. Even his school teachers loved him. I can certainly see why.

I did a lot of reading and researching about brain injuries while sitting in the waiting room at the hospital. I read in more than one place that light stimulation, familiar sounds and sights, and a familiar touch can do a lot of healing for a patient. Because of the donations made to us during this extremely difficult time, I was able to do a few things for Daniel that I felt were important. As I mentioned before, I purchased a clock radio for his CCU room. The radio stayed on in the background around the clock. We left the radio playing familiar music. Some of the nurses even commented that they would turn up the radio on their shift so that they could sing along. The music often lightened an otherwise dreary mood.

The basketball team Daniel helped coach sent him a plaque with a team picture on it as a way to encourage Daniel. I also went to a local pharmacy and had many pictures printed and taped them on the walls in Daniel's CCU room. Daniel's therapists even used some of those pictures as part of his therapy when trying to get him to respond, point, reach, or shake his head. I also purchased soft balls from the toy section at a store. I was determined that Daniel could squeeze them and build the strength in his hands. The first thing he did when I placed one in his hand was squeeze down on it, and then he rubbed his fingers over it to feel the texture. Positive stimulation was so important.

Daniel's visitors were somewhat restricted to immediate family, but we took several friends back at different times once we were sure Daniel could handle additional visitors. We made a point to keep our voices at a normal volume, talk about normal things, talk directly to Daniel (even if his eyes were closed), and always hold his hands. Daniel heard and understood much more than he responded to. For example, his parents and I were whispering once because we thought Daniel was asleep. His dad then made a comment that Daniel was probably hearing us and just playing opossum. About that time, Daniel, with his eyes closed, got a little smirk on his face and mumbled, "Uh huh."

I can remember so clearly a day that Daniel's mom was holding his left hand and I was holding his right hand. Daniel felt his mom's ring on her finger and started spinning it around and around with his fingers.

Eventually, he stopped spinning the ring and started trying to push it off her finger. Out of curiosity, we just watched and let him get the ring off. Before too long, he had the ring off of her finger and in his left hand. He tried to put the ring in his right hand, but his arms were still restrained to the bed. Somehow, after trying for a few seconds, he got the ring in his right hand, found my hand again, and put the ring on my finger. We were all amazed. I leaned down and asked him if that was his way of proposing marriage to me. He didn't say no, so I said yes! That gave us all a good laugh, which we needed desperately.

Daniel's mother's ring on Meredith's middle finger.

January 22—Dothan, Alabama (Facebook Update)
Daniel has a miniature Alabama football helmet that he bought this Christmas just for fun. When I came back from Troy yesterday I brought it with me to put in his room. He saw it this morning and apparently liked it. I told him it would give him something pretty to look at and he nodded his head. Roll Tide!

He played with the rings on his mom's and my hands again. He got the ring off his mom's hand, switched it to his other hand and put it on my finger! A proposal maybe? Ha! We loved it!!!

I am very pleased with his progress this morning. We still have several prayer requests but God is hearing and answering! Pray for the swelling to continue to decrease. Pray for his fever to stay away.

Pray for his Nurse, Deeanna, to be alert and on point today. Pray for the blood cultures to show no infection, bacteria or viruses. Pray that the ventilator weaning process will go well and he will keep what little strength he has. Pray that the damage to his frontal lobes will heal completely! God is SO good!!!

Chapter 9

Over the next few days, everything stayed status quo. Early one morning, a doctor entered the waiting room where we were sleeping and called out Daniel's family name. His parents and I woke up with quite a start. Dr. McNeal, another neurosurgeon, had been in to evaluate Daniel and wanted to speak to his family. He was very pleased with Daniel's progress. For the first time in almost eight days, a doctor said two very important words:

Meredith with daughter, Addison.

"He's stable." Praise the Lord! Having heard that great news, even before 7:00 a.m., we were wide awake and already thanking God for a beautiful day of blessings that could only come from Him.

Daniel hit another big milestone that day. The doctors all agreed that he was ready to have the ventilator removed. It was a big day for me too. My parents brought my daughter to Dothan so that I could take her to Chuck-e-Cheese and spend time with her outside the hospital. We both needed that time.

While Addison and I were eating pizza and playing games, across town at the hospital, the doctors were taking Daniel off the ventilator. I remember getting a text from Daniel's mother that said, "Nurse just came to get us. Said somebody is asking for us." I hated so badly that I was not there, but spending that uninterrupted time with my daughter was so important. By the next visitation hour, I was back at the hospital. It was so great to see my handsome Daniel's face without the tubes and tape attached. His color was great, and his vitals were strong. He was breathing well on his own.

My dad went back with me to see Daniel. He and my mom had both been by my side daily since Daniel's accident. When he got ready to leave, he told Daniel he wanted to shake his hand. Daniel let go of my hand, reached up to my dad, gripped his hand, and actually shook it up and down a little. The Lord really revealed himself that day in ways that were obvious to everyone.

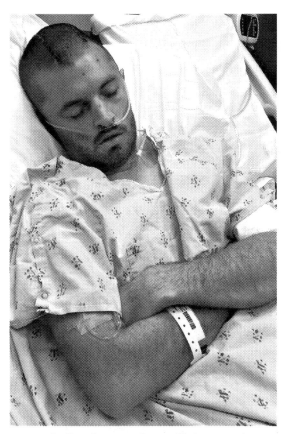

Daniel after being taken off the ventilator.

January 23—Dothan, Alabama (Facebook Update)

Y'all … I'm struggling for words to describe the joy in my heart right now! If you can't look at all God has done in Daniel's life over the past 12 days and know how BIG and how GOOD He is, and how much He LOVES us … Then you've been blinded by Satan himself and have hardened your heart.

Praises! Daniel has been extubated and is breathing well on his own! His blood cultures all came back negative! Daniel is able to speak! Daniel is stable!

Prayer Requests: That we will have a night nurse who is godly and good with neuro patients. That Daniel will rest and get stronger throughout the next days, continuing to breath on his own. That the swelling will continue to decrease in his brain and that the frontal lobe damage will heal completely. That Daniel will be patient and determined, persevering throughout the days to come. That we will know how to best minister to Daniel. Thank You, Lord! Your mercies are new every morning!

"O Lord, you are my God; I will exalt you and praise your name, for in perfect faithfulness you have done marvelous things, things planned long ago" (Isaiah 25:1 NIV).

Chapter 10

January 23—Dothan, Alabama (Facebook Update)

Last update for the night. I'm fading fast! It's been a day full of emotions. Anxiety, fear, joy, excitement … But God brought this all together, put it all in place for us to glorify Him and give Him all of our praise! He, and only He, can do what has been done in Daniel's life. God, and only God, can make known the ways and use the doctors as tools to accomplish what has been done in Daniel's life. We are not worthy, but we are loved!

Daniel is doing well tonight. Kris is our nurse again tonight. You have no idea how happy that makes "the girlfriend." He talked to us a lot about what all he had done with Daniel in the short hour he had been there. Daniel is answering addition and multiplication problems. He looks at and recognizes pictures. There is some deficit with the vision in his right eye, but we were expecting that to some degree as a result of the stroke.

I heard some of the sweetest words tonight, straight from Daniel's mouth. "I need you." "I love you." Thank you, sweet Jesus! Music to my ears!

That same day, we had some pretty detailed and emotional discussions about where Daniel would go for rehabilitation. We all felt strongly that Daniel should go to Shepherd Center in Atlanta, Georgia. Shepherd Center is known nationwide for providing the best brain injury, stroke, and spinal cord rehabilitation. Daniel, obviously, was dealing with both brain injury and stroke. It is the only rehabilitation hospital to have Intensive Care and Acute Care Units.

One of the biggest frustrations we experienced came when realizing that we had to wait for Workers' Compensation to do their own research and tell us where they would pay for Daniel to go. Having the health, well-being, and future of my Daniel be in limbo because of a big corporate insurance company did not sit well with me. It was at that point that I became more vocal about what we, as a family, wanted for Daniel's future.

January 24—Dothan, Alabama (Facebook Update)

Just saw my handsome Daniel again! He is doing really well. More blood work is being done just to follow up on some virus suspicions, but his temp is still normal and he is still stable!

The Speech Therapist still has not come today. She usually comes late in the afternoons according to Daniel's nurse, Drew. They will repeat the swallow test at that time. The Pulmonary Specialist decided to go ahead and put Daniel back on fluids so that he doesn't get dehydrated. He decided not to put in an NG tube just yet so that Speech Therapy will have a chance to work with Daniel over the next day or two. Hopefully we can avoid the NG tube all together.

Some mention has been made about moving toward rehab pretty soon now that Daniel is off the ventilator. Please continue to pray in this regard. Pray that Workers Comp will work with us as we really feel Shepherd Center is the place Daniel needs to be.

I bought two spongey balls today for Daniel to squeeze. He loves the feel of our rings and fingernails, so I thought that might give him some entertainment without being a potential harm.

Please continue to pray! God hears and answers our prayers!

Beginning that very same day, I prayed that God would open the hearts and minds of not only the doctors, but also the Workers' Compensation case managers, and put things in place for Daniel to be accepted and transferred to Shepherd Center. I prayed specifically that God would deal with Workers' Compensation and make Shepherd Center their best and only option for Daniel. First, I talked to God. Second, I talked to Daniel's parents. Next, I talked to the doctors. Then, we told Workers' Compensation what we wanted for Daniel. It soon became apparent that all of Daniel's doctors were on board with our wishes. Then we waited for a final decision from Workers' Compensation.

Chapter 11

To say that my heart sunk would be an understatement. The next day, I rounded the corner into Daniel's room, and he was missing from his bed. The man I love had been unconscious or semi-conscious, restrained, undergone two major surgeries, and now he was not where I last left him. Cue the panic attack! It took me several seconds to process that Daniel wasn't in his bed … because he was reclining in a chair! That's right, a chair! Sitting pretty in his bright blue safety helmet was my Daniel. Before you get too excited, he was still pretty much sleeping the whole time. It still took major effort for him to open his eyes. But the physical therapists had come and moved him to a chair for several hours in hopes of helping him regain his mobility as well as resetting his sleep-wake cycles. This was a huge step!

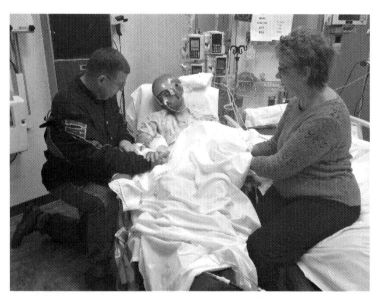

Daniel sitting up in the recliner.

January 25—Dothan, Alabama (Facebook Update)
This morning brought new mercies, indeed, just as God promised! We walked in and were a little startled when we didn't see Daniel in his bed. But we looked around the corner and found him sitting in a recliner! And he had been fitted for his new helmet that he will have to wear for safety any time he gets out of bed.

Physical Therapy had already been by. Occupational Therapy will come back later when he isn't so worn out from Physical Therapy. Speech Therapy will also come by today to reassess his ability to swallow, and work on his breath support for talking.

After lunch we will be contacting the Workers Comp Case Worker. Please be in prayer even now for her to be receptive to the family's desire to see Daniel go to Shepherd Center in Atlanta. We ask The Lord to pave the way for this and go ahead of us, as we know He does. Continue to pray, dear Prayer Warriors!

Later that same day, we met again with Dr. Passler, the neuropsychologist. Dr. Passler was very encouraged with his latest assessment. Daniel had progressed from a 3 to a 20 on the scale the doctor used to assess cognitive abilities and awareness. That was where the doctor wanted him to be. That number 20 had been a goal, and Daniel had reached it only by the grace of God.

Dr. Passler woke Daniel and asked him several questions. He had me talk to Daniel and get him to respond as well. Daniel, when asked who was talking to him, responded by saying, "my girlfriend." I was one happy girl. But in the very next breath, when asked my name, he called the wrong name, which confused and upset me. When prompted with the first letter of my name, he then got it right. The doctor explained that Daniel may be reverting to childhood or previous memories, and he should not be judged by that one statement. The doctor assured me that he would come around if he continued to progress at the rate he had been.

That very same day, while we visited with Daniel, a lady named Kelly came to meet with us in Daniel's room. Kelly, oh Kelly. God, oh

God. God, thank you for Kelly. You see, Kelly is an admissions liaison at Shepherd Center. She came to tell us that she had a room for Daniel and they were excited to work with him! Can you see God working this out? Really? God was all over it, directing each step of the process and lining things up so that we had nothing to worry about. Kelly spent more than an hour with us, showing us brochures and pictures of the facility, explaining how the process works with housing, and helping with anything else she thought we needed to know. Kelly gave us a lot of information. We had some questions about being able to participate in therapy with Daniel to keep him encouraged. She was able to answer all of our questions. When she left, we were overwhelmed with information and gratitude. Shepherd Center wanted to work with my Daniel, and they came to us to prove it. From that point on, no mention was made about any other rehabilitation facility. Shepherd Center was our destination. Another answer to our very specific prayers.

> **January 25—Dothan, Alabama (Facebook Update)**
> **Affirmation that God is all over this!!! No sooner than I posted my update from the morning visit, and requested prayer about Workers Comp being willing to work with us and get Daniel to Shepherd Center, Mrs. Wanda [Daniel's mother] motioned for me to come out into the hallway. I went out to talk to her and she told me that a lady named Kelly from Shepherd Center had left her a voicemail, and she was on her way to Dothan to meet with us about Daniel at 2pm. Um, hello??? Thank you, Lord!!! Now we just have to get Workers Comp on board because Shepherd Center is ready for Daniel!**

After our meetings with Dr. Passler and with Kelly, I was emotionally spent. One thing that Kelly told us was that as a part of daily therapies, they used timers. She said that each patient had a timer, and some had multiple timers, to help them with daily tasks. Timers went off around the clock as a part of therapy for most patients. The thought of my Daniel needing multiple timers to help him function was more than I could bear.

So I prayed. I prayed that God would heal Daniel and cause him to not need the intimidating timers, beepers, lights, and sounds of the hospital to help him progress and become fully functional again. I just knew that God was listening. He is faithful. He is the Great Physician. He would do this for Daniel.

Chapter 12

January 26—Dothan, Alabama (Facebook Update)
Reading about Traumatic Brain Injury this morning as I wait to see Daniel. I won't lie … This is overwhelming! Lord be with us …

It wouldn't be much longer before the doctors moved Daniel out of CCU and into a room on the neurology floor of the hospital. The move up two floors was quite an ordeal. You see, we had basically made a home in the corner of the CCU waiting room. We had baskets, and baskets, and baskets of food, drinks, and puzzle books. We had blankets, pillows, luggage, and more that had to be cleaned out of the waiting room. I purchased a collapsible red wagon and storage containers. We loaded everything into the containers and loaded the containers into the wagon. We had so much leftover that we were able to leave bags of snacks in the waiting room for other families to enjoy. That was the least we could do since many of those families had become like family to us during this trial, this journey.

Wagon full of gifts.

Once we were settled on the neurology floor, Dr. Passler prescribed two medications to help reset Daniel's sleep-wake cycle. Having been in the CCU for two whole weeks, Daniel spent most of his time sleeping, and his brain didn't know when he was supposed to be awake. The medications given to him would help straighten out his nights and days. It was our job to keep the lights on, the window blinds open, and the television on during the day to help Daniel try to wake up. Then at night, we turned down the lights, turned off the television, and tried to let Daniel sleep. Unfortunately, our efforts didn't always work, and Daniel was still asleep much of the day and awake a lot at night. But he was slowly coming around.

Over the next three days, things moved quickly. Daniel's staples were removed (all sixty-seven of them). Paperwork and insurance were finalized for Daniel's admission to Shepherd Center. His therapists started working a little harder with him, including letting him eat. He was given applesauce and crackers when working with speech therapy. The highlight of one of his days was when the speech therapist gave him a popsicle. She wanted him to eat it very slowly so that she could watch him swallow and make sure he didn't have any residual backing up that could cause him to choke or aspirate later. However, Daniel bit the popsicle in half and chewed it up like a champ. He finished the whole thing in three bites. I'd say he enjoyed that sweet treat.

Daniel's sister, Stephanie, and I sat with Daniel for a while in his new room. We just sat quietly, watching television and occasionally looking at Daniel to make sure he was not reaching for his feeding tube. Several times, we saw Daniel looking intently but quietly at the pictures on the walls, the calendar, and the posters drawn for him by my daughter, his niece, and his nephews. Those were the same pictures that had been hanging in Daniel's CCU room. Only now Daniel was aware enough to actually take interest in what he was seeing.

That same evening, Stephanie called home to check in. Her daughter, Daniel's niece, Sydney, answered the phone. Sydney and Daniel have a really special relationship. She is his only niece. At twelve years old, she was still running and jumping into Uncle Daniel's arms when she saw him. Their relationship is so special. That night, while she was on the phone, her mom put the phone up to Daniel's ear so that Sydney could tell him hello. Daniel responded to her by asking her what she was doing. When she replied that she was watching television, he said, "Shouldn't you be in bed?

It's late." That is when Stephanie took the phone back so that she could talk to Sydney. Sydney was crying happy tears because her Uncle Daniel was able to talk to her. He was healing a little more every day.

"I love you too, Honey." Those are some of the sweetest words I had heard in over two weeks. As I got ready to leave the hospital that night to go to the hotel, I leaned down to kiss Daniel, and he puckered his lips and kissed me back. That in itself was a big deal. Then I told him I loved him. He replied by saying, "I love you too, Honey." You see, he had always called me "Honey" as a term of endearment. I had missed hearing that and knowing that he said it without being prompted, knowing that his memory and mind were coming around, meant even more.

To top off the night, Daniel asked me what time it was before I left. I pointed across the room to where a clock was hanging on the wall. I asked him if he could tell me what time the clock reflected. After sitting there for a minute and concentrating on the clock, he said, "Nine." You know what? He was right! Another huge victory!

Daniel's parents roomed in with him after he was moved to the floor. I spent those next few nights sleeping in a real bed across the street from the hospital at a hotel. After I showered and crawled into bed that night, I picked up my Bible and began to read. I prayed and prayed for Daniel's healing. I also prayed that God would take my fears. Then God gave me a gentle reminder. "Have I not commanded you? Be strong and courageous. Do not be terrified; do not be discouraged, for the Lord your God will be with you wherever you go" (Joshua 1:9 NIV).

Chapter 13

The next two days of physical therapy got Daniel up and walking. He walked the entire length of the loop around the nurses' station with the help of the therapists. He had to be taught to keep a wide stance while walking rather than walking heel-to-toe. He did very well. He also worked well with his speech therapist by completing several shape puzzles, brushing his own teeth, eating and drinking, as well as naming animals.

That night, God screamed at me. You heard me. He screamed at me. "As for GOD, his way is perfect; the word of the Lord is flawless. He is a shield for all who take refuge in him" (Psalm 18:30 NIV). I promise I could hear Him saying, *I told you so. I've got this. Trust me. Let me work.* And that's exactly what He was doing. I had to remind myself to stay out of His way. I was reminded of the words of the hospital chaplain: "Sit on your hands if you have to."

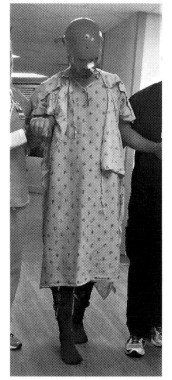

Daniel walking.

January 28—Dothan, Alabama (Facebook Update)

So thankful that Daniel had a good day. He worked well with PT and OT. Speech Therapy was more detailed today and he did well. He fed himself an entire cup of applesauce with no trouble. He is

drinking water from a straw and swallowing well. They will do one more swallow test before they pull the NG tube from his nose …

Daniel took a walk down the hall and back with PT today. He has good leg strength. We just have to work on wider foot positioning to give him more stability. He also completed three shape puzzles with no trouble today. He named animals when asked to, and read many words. I wrote out the Bible verse, Joshua 1:9 and let him read it. "Have I not commanded you? Be strong and courageous. Do not be terrified; do not be discouraged, forThe Lord your God will be with you wherever you go." He read it, and said he liked it.

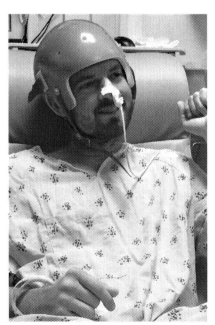

Daniel's first real smile.

The very next day, we got our first real smile out of Daniel. My mom and dad came to visit with us. My mom went to Daniel's side and reached for his hand. She made some comment about Alabama football and the next thing we noticed was a genuine smile on Daniel's face. He looked directly at my mom and smiled a big, toothy grin. Be still my heart! I thank God that I was able to snap a picture of that smile. I look back at the picture today and praise God for this huge blessing.

That was the same day that Daniel started showing a very clear sense of humor. He named each of the people in the room, but when he came to one of his nephews, he said, "I don't know. I don't think I am related to him." For a brief second we all sat stunned. I turned to glance at Daniel and noticed a little smirk on his face. He knew exactly who his nephew was, and he was joking with him. That moment of internal panic on my part was turned into laughter within seconds. *I've got this. Trust me. I'm working.*

January 28—Dothan, Alabama (Facebook Update)
As our night winds down I sit here reflecting on everything the day held. This morning Daniel slept a lot. He was taken down for one more Barium Swallow Test. The test showed that he is swallowing and not aspirating, however, he has a good bit of residual that could become an issue. So for now, the NG tube stays in and they will follow up with further testing at Shepherd Center.

Daniel walked with PT today and did a lot of upper body exercises with exercise bands. He ate a popsicle, brushed his teeth, drank some water, had lots of visitors, and stayed awake a lot of the day. I have been SO proud of him. He is my hero! He has had a big day. His short term memory is not good so we have to repeat ourselves a lot. But he is doing very well.

Please pray for the frontal lobe damage to heal completely! Pray for his memory. Pray for a good night of sleep and rest for his body, mind and spirit. Pray for safety as he is transported to Shepherd Center tomorrow morning. God has ordered every step of this journey so far and He will continue to do so!

The next day was a big day. We were all preparing mentally for the transition to rehabilitation. We had been told that Daniel would need clothes that he would be comfortable in for exercise and sleep. His parents and I knew that we would have to go to our homes and pack bags. We struggled greatly with the idea of Daniel arriving in Atlanta, a strange place, with a head injury that causes confusion anyway, and him not having one of us with him. I prayed over and over for God to provide a solution. God wasted no time answering this very specific prayer. That evening, before going to the hotel to shower and sleep, I received a text message from Daniel's brother, Ken, and his wife, Amanda. Ken had decided to take off work and drive to Atlanta on Friday morning to be there when Daniel arrived at Shepherd Center. This was such a relief for all of us. Daniel's mom cried happy tears and hugged me with a huge sigh of relief. Daniel would arrive at Shepherd Center, and his brother would be there waiting for him to be his support system and encourager until we could get there the next morning.

Daniel was awakened early that Friday morning to get a bath and get ready to be transported by ambulance to Shepherd Center in Atlanta. Daniel was insistent that he was getting a shower. He didn't want anyone bathing him. He wanted a shower. After his physical therapists finished their rounds with Daniel, we asked Clay, one of the therapists, if he would assist Daniel with a shower. Clay stayed and made sure Daniel was safe while in the shower. Then, Daniel was cold and tired and wanted to lie down in the bed. It wasn't long before he dozed off. All I wanted to do was crawl into the bed and snuggle with him. I laid against him with my head on his pillow and my forehead against his forehead, and I prayed. I prayed for healing. I prayed for safety. I prayed for guidance and wisdom for his caregivers and doctors. I just closed my eyes and prayed.

Meredith praying over Daniel.

January 29—Dothan, Alabama (Facebook Update)
I'm sitting here staring at the most handsome man.
He's snoring away. They came in this morning to bathe
him and he said he wanted a shower. So they helped
him get a shower, and he was a happy boy. He's snug
as a bug in a rug right now.

The closer the time comes to the ambulance
arriving, the more anxious I get. I don't want to leave
him. At all. I'm thankful that his brother, Ken, will
be making the trip to Atlanta today to help him get
settled in. Today, I will be going back to Troy to pack
Daniel's bags for rehab and I will travel to Atlanta
tomorrow morning. His parents will go home for the
night as well, and travel to Atlanta tomorrow.

Please pray for an easy transition for Daniel,
for safe travels for everyone, for complete recovery
and healing for Daniel! God is so good and we look
forward to watching this miracle progress. Keep
praying, y'all!!!

Around midmorning, the ambulance company arrived to pick up
Daniel and transport him to Atlanta. We all gathered our things and
followed Daniel out to the ambulance. We reminded him what was going
on and where he was going, and assured him that his brother, Ken, would
be there waiting for him at Shepherd Center. Once the ambulance pulled
out on to the highway, we got in our cars and headed home. I drove to
Troy, picked up my daughter, washed several loads of laundry, and packed
Daniel's belongings that he would need for rehab. Daniel's parents drove
to Greenville, washed laundry, repacked, and got some rest.

January 29—Dothan, Alabama (Facebook Update)
He's off to Shepherd Center! 18 days later I'm
leaving Dothan. It was about this same time (11:08am)
on January 12th that I got the call to come to Dothan
because Daniel had cut his hand …

Chapter 14

My first night away from Daniel since his accident was emotionally very difficult for me. I did not like being away from him. However, I desperately needed the time alone with my daughter to give us both a sense of normalcy. We went to dinner with my parents and enjoyed that time of fellowship. Since Daniel had moved into an apartment in Troy prior to his accident, it was up to me to gather what he would need and take it to him. So, after dinner, I packed Daniel's clothes that he would need for rehab, washed a load of laundry, watched a movie with Addison, and tried not to get emotional. That night, Addison snuggled up right against me, and we both slept soundly.

> **January 29—Troy, Alabama (Facebook Update)**
> **Please continue to pray for My Daniel. He got settled in at Shepherd Center around 3:00 this afternoon. He had to go through a thorough evaluation, some testing, and the doctor was pleased with where Daniel is and the progress he has made so far. Prayer works, folks! Don't stop now! Daniel still has swelling and damage to the frontal lobes that need healing. His body still needs rest. Please pray regarding his memory. His short term memory is basically nonexistent. Of the last 2 months he only remembers bits and pieces at best. His walking is still unsteady, even though his legs are strong. My God is bigger than all of the issues Daniel faces! I pray for complete healing!**

Atlanta is a three-hour drive for me. It is closer to a four-hour drive for Daniel's parents. That Saturday morning, I was determined that I was going to get to Atlanta early so that I could spend as much time as possible with Daniel. I asked my little girl if she wanted to go, but she did not. I dropped her off with my parents and drove nonstop to Atlanta.

When I arrived in Daniel's room at Shepherd Center, he was sound asleep. I didn't want to wake him, so I quietly put away his clothes and his shoes, hung pictures on the wall, and cleaned up in the room. I hung a calendar on Daniel's closet door. This was my best attempt to help Daniel regain a sense of time and date. As each day ended, we would draw a line on the calendar marking out the day. That way, when Daniel went to the closet to get his clean clothes each morning, he could see what day it was currently. No sooner than I was about to sit down, I heard, "Hey." I looked up and Daniel was awake. I walked over to his bed, sat on the edge, and we had our first real conversation in almost three weeks. I was with him a little more than an hour before his parents arrived.

January 30—Atlanta, Georgia (Facebook Update)

Well, folks, Daniel is sound asleep ... again. He did wake up for a while. He wasn't feeling his best. I think his stomach is the cause of him not feeling well. We talked, I read him some of the cards he had received, and I showed him the #teamdaniel bracelet I was wearing. He loved all of it. But he hates being the center of attention. Always has. My humble hero wants to get well, but doesn't want all of the focus on himself. I told him it was too bad because he didn't have a say in the matter this time!

His short term memory is still really bad. I was in the room with him for a while when I first got here. He slept most of the time, but occasionally would wake up and talk to me. Then, I left to walk down the hall, and his parents arrived. They asked him where I had gone, and he didn't remember me being there. But yet he still calls me "Honey," tells me he loves me, blows me kisses, returns my kisses, and we have completely normal conversations when he's awake. It seems that

his memory erases after he falls asleep and wakes up again.

Daniel did spend a few hours out of the bed. He is snoozing away at the moment. I wish he would wake up and watch this beautiful sunset. But I will let him rest. I love him. I wish I could do more than just sit here and hold his hand, rub his back, and sing. I want to make it all better. Time. Give it time, they all say. Patience is a virtue. We love our Prayer Warriors!

I roomed in with Daniel that night. It was quite an eventful night. Daniel pulled out his feeding tube. Twice. The nurses were not happy with him. Each time the tube had to be replaced down his nose and into his stomach, an X-ray had to be done to confirm proper placement. The more I think about it, that's just gross. Can you imagine what's in your stomach coming up through your nose?

On a cleaner, happier note, Daniel was very vocal, and his mind was clearer that night. When he wanted his hands unrestrained, he would wake me by loudly, calling my name, "Meredith!" I was just happy to hear the right name. After he pulled out the feeding tube the second time, he wanted his hands loosed. I told him that I would get in trouble if I untied them. He informed me that I would not get in trouble because he would lie and say he did it himself because I was asleep. I had never heard him so conniving and deceitful. Surely it was just the head injury talking.

The next day, Daniel had many visitors. His sister, Stephanie, her husband, Andy, and their children, Bryan and Sydney, came, and also brought a friend, Brittany. Daniel's brother, Ken, and his wife, Amanda, came and brought one of their sons, Daulton. Needless to say Daniel had a room full of love and encouragement. Saturdays and Sundays at Shepherd Center are more for rest than rehab. Established patients have a few therapy sessions early in the day on Saturday, but Sunday is a day of rest. Sundays are also a time of worship. Shepherd Center hosts a nondenominational worship service each Sunday. For our family, whose faith is grounded in God Almighty, this was very encouraging.

A small part of Daniel's cheering squad.

Daniel slept much of that Sunday. He would wake up occasionally to see who was in the room, respond to our questions, and participate in conversation. However, it was never long before his eyes were closed again and he was asleep. Daniel talked to my daughter on the phone for the first time since his accident. That meant so much to her. She needed to hear his voice and know that he still loved her and he would be okay.

I did not want to leave Daniel. I did not want to drive back home. I couldn't stand the thought of not seeing him until the next weekend. The more I thought about leaving, the more emotional I became. Finally, around 4:30 p.m., I forced myself to get up, gather my belongings, say my farewells, and leave Shepherd Center for home. Although I felt like I was leaving a piece of home behind. I cried all the way to the Alabama state line. Just before I arrived home, I received a text message from Daniel's niece, Sydney. It was a picture of her with Daniel. He was awake and smiling. We all needed to see that smile. Especially Daniel's Sydney.

Daniel and his niece, Sydney.

Chapter 15

Each day, we watched the swelling of Daniel's brain decrease. Each day, the sides of his head would sink in a little farther, making the piece of skull still in place in the center of his head more pronounced. Each weekend, I took pictures of Daniel's head and texted them to his neurosurgeon in Dothan so that he could follow the progress. This allowed the neurosurgeon to give us an approximate timeline for when he would replace the bone flaps. The bone flaps were being stored in sterile solution in a freezer at the hospital in Dothan, so Daniel would have to return to Dothan for the surgery when it was time. It was so encouraging to have responses from his neurosurgeon like, "He looks great," and, "Swelling is going down just like we want." God was continuing to work. He had provided the intimate connection through text messaging to let us know that we were not alone, and his doctor was only a few clicks away.

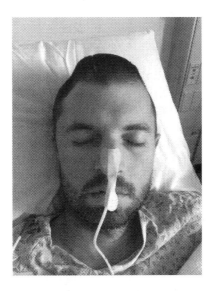

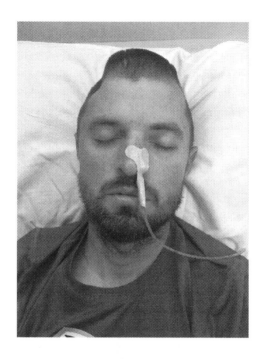

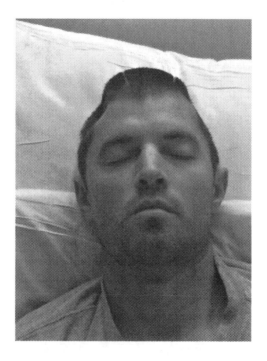

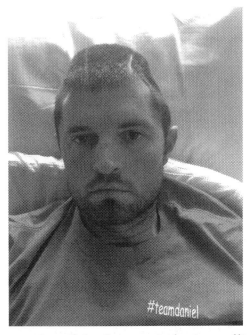

Progression of the decrease in brain swelling.

We were also blessed with great case managers both in Alabama and in Georgia. On many occasions, the Georgia case managers would come sit down with us, make notes, update us on what the current goals were for Daniel, and make sure we didn't need anything. I'm "the girlfriend." The case managers did not have to keep me in the loop, but they did. They treated me like I was Daniel's wife. Many times, they told me they could see in my eyes and actions how much he meant to me. This, my friends, was another answer to prayers. I did not want to be left out. I needed to be involved in every part of Daniel's care. Daniel's parents, doctors, and case managers all included me in every step of the journey.

Speaking of blessings, we had the best nurses in Dothan, and top-notch nurses at Shepherd Center as well. The sights, smells, and sounds of Shepherd Center were very different from those of the hospital in Dothan. Where we gained our sense of love and welcome came from the familiar smiles and encouraging words of the nurses. Daniel's dad affectionately named one of Daniel's rehab nurses "Drill Sergeant." Nurse Mary, aka Drill Sergeant, was one of a kind. She meant business, but she also knew when a smile or joke was needed.

My fondest memory of Nurse Mary was when she came into Daniel's room laughing one day. When we asked what was funny, she said she would tell us later. Apparently there were other inappropriate listening ears on the other side of the curtain where Daniel's roommate and his family were visiting. Eventually, she returned to Daniel's room and explained her laughter. A patient who was suffering a brain injury had caused quite a scene and put one of his nurses in a headlock. "All's well that ends well," and there was no harm done, so all was well. It was the laugh of the nurses' station, and we laughed along with them.

Physical therapy, speech therapy, occupational therapy, and recreational therapy would occupy Daniel's weekdays. We fully expected Daniel to face challenges. What we were not expecting were dizzy spells, drops in blood pressure, and increased heart rate. Daniel had major physical adjustments that had to be made due to the atmospheric pressure on his brain. Without his skull in place to protect him from those pressure changes, Daniel got dizzy, lightheaded, and sick to his stomach. This happened quite a bit. For a man who was never sick otherwise, these feelings were new for Daniel. Feeling bad only added to the frustration of cognitive difficulties and confusion he was experiencing.

To think back to a time when standing in two-minute intervals was a challenge is hard to believe. Standing was hard on its own, but it also started causing Daniel to experience headaches. The problem with Daniel's headaches was that he wouldn't realize he was hurting until the pain was so bad it made him sick. It took several days of monitoring him and his headaches before the doctor put him on a pain patch called Butrans. Daniel would wear them for one week at a time. These worked remarkably well for him in controlling pain and ultimately his nausea. He would also be given compression stockings and an abdominal binder to wear daily to help with balance. I prayed constantly for better days. "O Lord, be gracious to us; we long for you. Be our strength every morning, our salvation in time of distress" (Isaiah 33:2 NIV).

February 1—Troy, Alabama (Facebook Update)

I've been thinking about the prayers God has so specifically answered over the past 3 weeks. There are so many that I'm having to really sit back and read

my handwritten journal to be able to grasp it all. Can we ever really grasp it? I have wondered several times lately if I have limited God and what He wants to do in and through my life by trying to take control. Well, no more. He has showed up and showed out over the last 3 weeks and I know He won't stop now! God has great plans for My Daniel and I plan on having a front row seat!

When I got off work today I wanted to automatically pick up my phone and call Daniel, like I have done hundreds of times before. I wanted to let him know I was off work and headed to get supper and groceries. I wanted to ask him if I could pick up something for him to eat and find out what time I could expect him for dinner.

When I was grocery shopping I ran into several people who asked about Daniel, people who are following his recovery on Facebook. I can't tell you all how much that means to me. There are simply no words. When I got outside I had a complete come-apart and crying meltdown. Moments later, I received a phone call from Daniel's dad. Within seconds I heard the sweetest sound - Daniel's voice. We only talked for a few minutes. He said some very important words – "I miss you. I love you, Honey." He sure knows how to melt my heart!

Please pray for his doctors and therapists. Pray for his nurses and the techs who are also ministering to Daniel. Pray that Daniel's vision will be healed. Pray that the frontal lobe damage will be healed and the swelling will continue to decrease. Pray that Daniel's BP will stabilize when he stands and participates in PT. Pray that Daniel's swallow will improve so that the NG tube can be removed. God hears and He answers! Don't limit God in what He wants to do in your lives! Know that He can - He loves us!

Once his balance, headaches, and nausea were under control, Daniel's days were pretty routine. He would get up, shower, get dressed, eat breakfast, go to one or two of his therapy sessions, eat lunch, have one or two more sessions, and then go to his room until supper time. While his schedule was routine, his individualized therapies changed daily. Some days he pushed himself in the wheelchair to the store just down the street where he bought macaroni and cheese with his therapist. Other days, he had to go to the pharmacy across the street to do a scavenger hunt. Some days, he stayed indoors and played board games or video games that utilized strategy and problem-solving skills. He was required to do a lot of endurance and balance testing in physical therapy before he could graduate out of his wheelchair.

One thing we never got concerned about was Daniel's appetite. From the moment he was given real food and no longer needed the feeding tube, he cleaned his plate at every meal. Bacon, eggs, sausage, salad, hamburger steak, mashed potatoes, or spaghetti—it didn't matter what you put on his plate. Each meal provided nutrition, which gave him strength to complete his therapies.

February 2—Troy, Alabama (Facebook Update)
Last update for the night. The results of Daniel's vestibular testing came back negative – no vertigo! Hopefully the dizziness was just a result of his BP dropping because of him being in bed so long and trying to stand too quickly.

Daniel ate a big supper! Hamburger steak, green beans, some of a baked potato, and a roll! He also drank his Ensure. I'm so proud of him! Please continue to pray for My Daniel! Baby steps. Giant leaps. All a result of God's love for us!

Chapter 16

One of the hardest things for me was to be three hours away during the week and not getting to see firsthand the things that God was accomplishing in Daniel through therapy. I wanted so badly to be a part of every step. I relied heavily on Daniel's parents to talk to me daily and let me know what was going on and how Daniel was feeling. They probably got tired of seeing my phone number come up on their phones because I called several times each day. Daniel's mom was also very good about updating Daniel's calendar with daily accomplishments so that I could look at it each weekend. Not only was Daniel's progress of great concern to me, but we had hundreds, and maybe thousands, of prayer warriors from all over the world who wanted daily updates. They wanted to know what to pray for and what praises to sing about to God. We simply could not have gotten through this journey without the love, support, and prayers of every single one of our prayer warriors.

Daniel received cards daily from friends, loved ones, and some complete strangers. The deacons from our church also sent flowers to brighten up his room. Several friends made the trip to Atlanta just to encourage Daniel in his recovery. Daniel will tell you that for the first month of rehab, he didn't feel like himself. There was a lot of confusion about where he was, why he was there, and what he was doing. He simply didn't feel like Daniel. But seeing the familiar smiles and hearing the voices of friends and family made that strange feeling a little more bearable. We never left Daniel alone long enough to get upset or scared. We felt that the least we could do was provide a small sense of comfort by simply being there with him.

God placed constant reminders in our paths and in our hearts that He was with us. He provided for the every need of those who were helping to care for Daniel. His parents were fortunate enough to be able to take as much time as they needed away from their jobs to do what they needed to do for Daniel. With the support that we received from our loved ones and prayer warriors, we never had to worry about how things were going to get accomplished back at home. We knew that whatever needed to be done would get done. The house was being cared for. The bills were getting paid. Family was in good health. All we had to do was care for Daniel.

It would be three days shy of one month before my daughter would get to see Daniel after his accident. Because of her young age, she was never allowed to go into the CCU at the hospital in Dothan. She was, however, allowed to visit at Shepherd Center. The weekend she chose to go to Atlanta with me, we arrived late on a Saturday evening. Daniel was sound asleep. At first, I was confused and concerned because Daniel was sleeping on his stomach. Up until this time, Daniel was restricted to sleeping on his back because of the skull flaps that had been removed. However, his nurse that night assured me that at that point in Daniel's recovery, his brain had decreased in swelling enough that he was in no danger sleeping on his stomach unless he hit his head on the bedrails. If he was more comfortable and getting more sleep on his stomach, we wanted that for him. So we kept the bedrails covered with pillows and let him sleep. Addison and I spoke briefly to Daniel's parents that night, and then we walked over to the apartment to get some rest.

February 6 · Atlanta, GA · 👥

I'm here!!!!! And I don't care if he's asleep! I'M
HERE!!! 😍🖤😍🖤😍🖤😍🖤😍🖤😍🖤

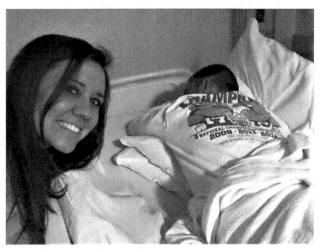

Facebook Post after arriving in Atlanta.

The next morning, Addison and I got up early and made our way to Daniel's room, but he had already gone to eat breakfast. We went to find him, and as we walked down the hallway to where he was, he turned his head and watched us approach. You could see the moment of recognition in his eyes. I wish I had snapped a picture. When we got to his table, he unlocked his wheelchair, backed up, and turned himself toward us. He grabbed ahold of my sweet little girl, pulled her to him, and embraced her with more love than I can describe. We spent that day playing games. Addison had no mercy on Daniel, but he didn't need it. They both won and lost some games. But I won something even greater than a game that day. Seeing him in his blue helmet, and even without it when the shape of his head was different, never phased Addison. He was just Daniel. And Daniel never skipped a beat in his relationship with her. This, my dear friends, was a God moment about which I prayed so deeply!

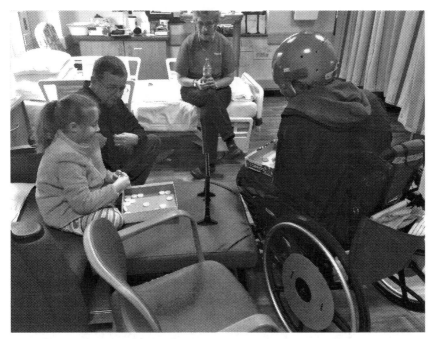

Daniel playing Connect Four with Meredith's daughter, Addison.

My God is forever faithful. He too never skips a beat in His relationship with us. I sometimes hear of people who have drifted away from the Church and from their relationship with Christ. That's just it. You see,

God is constant. He never moves away from us. We are the ones who distance ourselves from Him. He remains steady. It often takes a tragedy or trial in a person's life to make them realize the distance they have created between them and our loving God. I'm guilty of that very thing. No, I wasn't a terrible person. I was active in church and loved serving others. But my focus had drifted away from serving God rather than just serving in the church and fulfilling an obligation.

God opened my eyes to a lot of things when Daniel got hurt. I was sure I was losing everything, including my sanity. Then God reminded me Who is supposed to be my everything. It was time to refocus. I needed to become more like-minded with Christ and align my will, my purpose, and my desires with His will, purpose, and desires for my life. If I wanted God to do big things, I needed to return the effort.

Standing hugs. Best Valentine's Day gift.

Several weeks into his rehabilitation at Shepherd Center, Daniel began feeling a little more settled. He had gotten into a good routine. His sleep-wake cycles had reset and were normal. It was Valentine's weekend. I showed up in Atlanta with cards, candies, an Alabama National Championship shirt, and other special surprises for my Valentine. No, I wasn't upset that I didn't receive flowers or candies. I received something even better. For the first time in almost a month and a half, Daniel hugged me while standing. Yes, I was supporting him a good bit, and his nurse was standing close by. But he was standing, his arms were wrapped around me, he was smiling, and I have a picture to prove it! That was the very best gift I could have received from him on that Valentine's Day.

Another very important thing that happened that Valentine's weekend was that I got Daniel to bundle up and go outside. He needed fresh air. That was the first time he had been outdoors in over a month, with the exception of an ambulance ride to Shepherd Center. It is amazing what a little fresh air and sunshine can do to lift a person's spirits. The decrease in brain swelling may have begun to clear his ability to process things, but the bright sun and cool breeze on Daniel's face helped to refresh his mind.

The next weekend when I was visiting, he asked me about his cell phone. That was a big mental step in my opinion (because I'm a professional and all). Daniel had not had his cell phone, or even asked for it, in more than a month. I had his cell phone in my purse, but kept it turned off. About every three days or so I would turn it on, let it update, and then turn it back off. Occasionally I turned it on to pay his bill, and then turned it off again. That particular weekend, I just so happened to have charged his phone before driving to Atlanta.

Cell phone usage by patients was not highly recommended. Many patients with brain injuries who used cell phones would not realize what they were doing or remember what they would post on social media. The fear was that they would post something that they would later regret or make them embarrassed, or something that could get them in trouble. But this particular day, I pulled Daniel's phone out of my purse, turned it on for him, and gave it to him. The first thing he did was pull up the ESPN app. After a few minutes, he looked at Facebook and then Twitter. Not once did he try to post anything on social media, text anyone, or make any phone calls. We didn't really have great concerns about what he would do with his phone, so I left it for him and made him promise to call and text me as often as he could. We didn't, however, tell anyone other than family that he had his phone. We didn't want his phone to constantly be ringing or alarming with incoming messages that he would feel needed answers or replies.

I very vividly remember the first text message I got from Daniel after his accident. "I love you! Be careful." That was the text I received after I left him in Atlanta that first Sunday evening after he asked for his phone. I also remember the first time I looked down at my ringing phone and saw his name. I cried like a little baby. I remember thinking that I may never hear his voice again or receive another text from him. Then, a little later in this journey, to hear his sarcasm come back into play, caused me to cry again. It was a Wednesday, February 24, to be exact, when I breathed a sigh of relief. As I was talking to Daniel, I asked him how he was feeling. He replied with three of the sweetest words: "I'm feeling good." There was a reassurance in his voice that is forever imprinted in my mind. My Daniel was healing. My Daniel was still in there. My Daniel would be the same after as he was before the accident. And My *God* was doing it all!

Daniel's physical therapist knew that he loved basketball. Throughout the weeks, one of her personal goals was to get him in the basketball gym. A few weeks into rehab, once Daniel regained better balance, his therapist took him to the gym. It quickly became evident that while he was very confident dribbling and handling the basketball, his shooting skills were very off. Daniel doesn't miss free throws. And Daniel missed free throws. His depth perception was greatly affected by the changes in his vision as a result of his stroke in the left occipital region of his brain. Once the therapist and Daniel's dad told him to change his position and just aim at the backboard, he began making shots. On a funny note: It is an absolutely natural reaction for a basketball player to lunge for a ball if it bounces off the rim toward the side. Automatically, Daniel lunged after one of the balls. His physical therapist almost freaked out because she thought he was going to fall. Thankfully, he didn't fall. But I'm pretty sure that therapist had to restart her heart and regroup after that happened.

February 24—Troy, Alabama (Facebook Update)
Daniel has had another great day! He got to shoot some hoops today! He shot from the free throw line and

hit several shots, but many came up short. If you know My Daniel, you know that he doesn't miss free throws. I imagine this frustrated him to some degree. Most likely this is all a result of his vision being affected by the occipital stroke. Again, he has very little vision in his right eye. Please pray that he will heal and regain his sight! He WILL play basketball again with the strength, confidence and ability he had before!

Daniel is rooming in with his parents in the Transitional Living apartment in the hospital tonight and tomorrow night. Please pray that everything continues to go well and that the transition is smooth for his projected inpatient discharge on Saturday. Every day is a new adventure. Every day brings new healing. Every day brings new promises. Lamentations 3:22-23 reminds us that, "Because of the Lord's great love we are not consumed, for his compassions never fail. They are new every morning; great is your faithfulness." God continues to show up in ways we were never expecting. Please continue your prayers for My Daniel! He's SO worth it!

Chapter 17

Some days, we felt like Daniel was taking giant leaps in a positive direction with his recovery. Other days, we felt like he was stuck. But at least "stuck" wasn't going backward, right? I remember thinking that Daniel was acting depressed. Some days I would ask him how he was feeling, and he would say, "Terrible," but would be unable to tell me exactly why. At times, I told him, "You're doing great," and he would respond by saying, "Unfortunately." I never felt like he wanted to give up, but there were times when I knew I had to do something to pull him out of his slump. I refused to let depression set in and take over his recovery.

One weekend, I made strawberry cupcakes with strawberry icing, one of Daniel's favorites. When I walked into his room, I put the cupcakes in his lap and told him to cheer up. That boy had the nerve to ask me if I made the cupcakes, like he wasn't going to eat any if I didn't make them. Of course I made the cupcakes. At the moment, he didn't want to eat one so I put them on a table in the corner. I'm not sure how many he actually ate, but I'm pretty sure one of his nurses helped clean them out. We also had a little yellow box of bite-size candy bars that we called "Nurse Bait." I think they liked the treats we brought into Daniel's room. Happy, cheerful nurses make a difference in your patient's care. Take care of your nurses, and they will take care of you.

Another thing that was vital to Daniel's mental health throughout his rehabilitation, again, was fresh air. Between January 12 and January 29, Daniel did not see the light of day except through windows. On January 29, he was taken by ambulance from Dothan to Atlanta, only getting fresh air while loading and unloading the ambulance. At Shepherd Center in Atlanta, it was a few weeks into Daniel's rehab until we could take him off of the second floor, where his room and his nurses were located. The nurses had to evaluate Daniel and also give certain instructions to us about safety and emergency measures before we could take Daniel to another floor in the hospital.

Once we received the green light to take Daniel off of the second floor, I took him straight to the Secret Garden. This garden is an area outside of Shepherd Center with flower gardens, small fish ponds, water fountains, and sitting areas. It is a beautiful place where you can just sit and enjoy nature and the sounds of the crazy Atlanta life. The weather was still a bit chilly, but in my "professional opinion," Daniel needed the chill of the air to hit his face and wake him up a bit. He needed to remember the sights and sounds of the outdoors. We didn't stay long. Mission accomplished.

Daniel's niece, Sydney, nephew, Bryan, and Meredith's daughter, Addison, in the garden.

Another place in Shepherd Center where we spent a lot of time was in the Family Lounge. Daniel has quite the large cheering section, so when we all gathered at once, there was not room enough for all of us in his room. The Family Lounge had plenty of seating, a television, an area where children could play or watch movies, DVDs to be borrowed, a coffee pot, a vending machine, and a microwave. It also had one wall that was covered in huge windows, letting in a lot of light. The first few times we ventured to the Family Lounge, Daniel would doze off in his wheelchair. After several weeks, he stayed awake to enjoy his company and the change of scenery.

Across the parking deck in the residential building, there was another place we loved to spend time. On the Plaza Level of the residential building, there was an area where we played pool, foosball, and ping pong, and watched television on the big-screen TV. Outside the doors of the Plaza Level was a beautiful garden with walking paths, grills, and tables. There was also a mockingbird. This mockingbird was very aggressive. Daniel and I were walking the paths with his parents one afternoon, and the mockingbird was dive-bombing into our heads. My guess is that it was protecting a nest that we couldn't see. Needless to say, we stayed out of that garden the rest of that day. As a contribution and show of appreciation, we donated several packages of new ping pong balls, as well as four new pool cues to replace the ones that had been well loved (if you know what I mean).

Daniel playing pool with his nephew, Daulton.

Chapter 18

I mentioned before that Daniel had to endure balance testing before he could pass his physical therapy goals. Sometime in late February, Daniel passed his balance testing. This was such a praise! He passed with flying colors. He would have passed with 100 percent but when told to turn around, he turned toward the back and stopped, rather than turning in a complete circle. Who cares! He passed!

After his balance testing was completed, his parents and I were checked off to be able to walk with Daniel. This allowed us to help him in and out of the bed, walk down the hallway or to the bathroom, and exercise his legs. The physical therapist told us that we should let Daniel walk as much as possible and not use his wheelchair. I told her to take that wheelchair and get it out of his room. It was no longer an option. Daniel now had us to help him walk. I told him that he would not take that wheelchair to outpatient rehab. He would walk. And he did. Daniel never used that wheelchair again. Sometimes the girlfriend had to show a little tough love. But it got things done.

I'm no pro at handling hospital situations. I have no expertise when it comes to tragedy. I do, however, have the personality that says, "Handle it; you can grieve later." Every single day of Daniel's recovery, my mental status was, "Handle it," or "Make it happen." It was usually in the quiet of the night that I broke down and allowed myself to be vulnerable. While I realize that being emotional is expected of someone who has a loved one going through a trial like this, I also know that it is not in my nature to let anyone know when I'm grieving. A lot of my tears were shed laying on the floor in my bedroom. A lot of my anxiety had to be processed while I was sitting at my desk, trying to work. But every time, through prayer and petitions, I made my heart known to God. And just like His Word tells us, He did not fail me.

My expectations for Daniel's care and recovery have been, and remain, very high. I learned through the hospitalization of my grandmother in 2010 that you are your patient's best advocate. You know your patient better than the nurses and doctors. If you don't pay attention to the fine print and details, your patient can become just another chart, just another number. When that happens, you can bet your last dollar that your patient will become depressed and will lose their drive to get better. My Daniel was not going to become complacent. My Daniel was not going to be just another patient. My Daniel would get the best, most attentive care possible. If it took me exercising his fingers, arms, and legs, or scratching his back and massaging his shoulders, my Daniel would know that he was being taken care of, and his nurses would know that they were under the watchful, but grateful, loving eye of the girlfriend.

In many ways, God is the same way. He has a plan. He has high expectations. He loves us unconditionally. He is our safety net and guardian when nobody else seems to be watching out for us. Psalm 3:3, NIV, says, "But you, Lord, are a shield around me, my glory, the One who lifts my head high." God wants us to be encouraged. Sometimes that encouragement comes from those who love you. For those who are saved, who love the Lord and have committed their lives to him, the Holy Spirit will always encourage and convict you. The Lord, God, will protect you and be your shield in a life on this earth of the unknown. *Keep trusting in Me.*

On Saturday, February 27, Daniel graduated from inpatient rehabilitation to the outpatient program at Shepherd Pathways. This meant Daniel no longer stayed in a room in the hospital area of Shepherd Center, but rather in the apartment provided by Shepherd Center where his parents had been residing. That morning, we loaded up a cart full of Daniel's clothes, pictures, cards, flowers, and more, and Daniel walked out of Shepherd Center, leaving the wheelchair behind for good. It was almost like I could hear God saying, *I told you so.*

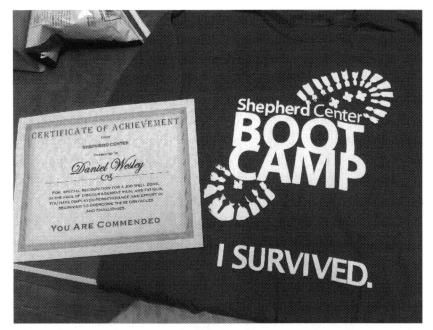

Daniel's certificate and shirt from inpatient therapy graduation

We celebrated Daniel's graduation that day by walking several blocks up the street to a restaurant and having a nice dinner. We picked up ice cream on the way back to the apartment and enjoyed that for dessert. I didn't realize until that day how much I had missed some of the little things. I got to walk down the street with my boyfriend, holding his hand, just like we had done so many times before. I got to sit down at a restaurant with him, order food, eat, and hold a conversation with him. I got to sit on a couch, snuggled up next to him, while we flipped through the television channels looking for something to watch. Oh, Lord, please let me never take that for granted ever again. It was times like that, feeling so grateful and normal, that made it difficult to return home to Alabama. I never liked leaving him behind. I always looked forward to the weekend ahead.

February 28—Troy, Alabama (Facebook Update)
Good evening, Prayer Warriors! I have had a wonderful weekend with My Daniel and now I'm home with my baby girl! Saturday, Daniel was discharged from inpatient therapy at Shepherd Center and we

got to spend the whole day outside of the hospital, walking the streets of Atlanta, and sitting down at a nice restaurant. We were celebrating a huge milestone! Daniel continues to eat like a champ! His sleep/wake cycle is finally on track.

Last night, Daniel got to sleep in a room that was not in a hospital. There were no beeps. There were no pump alarms. There were no bright lights at ungodly hours of the night. There were no sounds of trach suctioning. There was just silence. Peaceful silence for the first night in almost 7 weeks. That's right, this coming Tuesday was 7 weeks ago that Daniel's accident happened.

Chapter 19

Outpatient rehabilitation was another ballgame in itself. A new program meant new therapists, a new counselor, and a new doctor. We also gained yet another case worker. After initial evaluation at Shepherd Pathways, new goals were set for Daniel. His therapists and the doctor were both very encouraged by how far he had come, but they wanted to push him to be even better. Every program will have its bumps and quirks, but the Shepherd programs, hands down, are top notch. The doctor continued to monitor Daniel each week, watching closely to make sure he was progressing in the right direction. She referred him to an eye doctor for additional testing on his vision so that they could work together in that regard as well. Individual and group therapies were a part of Daniel's outpatient rehabilitation, and each served a very important purpose. Mental stimulation, cognitive advancement, physical healing, and communication skills were major goals at this point in Daniel's journey.

The Shepherd Pathways facility was off-campus from the main Shepherd Center. Since Daniel's injury happened at work, it was up to Workers' Compensation to provide transportation for Daniel from his temporary residence to therapy, and back home each day. I have heard a lot about how wonderful Uber is around the country. My personal opinion is that Uber is a hassle and a headache. Rarely did the scheduled transportation arrive on time. Many of the drivers, even with their GPS, did not know how to get to the destinations. Thank goodness for Pablo. Pablo was the one driver who was dependable, on time, personable, and helpful. Too bad he wasn't always the driver scheduled. Thankfully, Daniel and his parents always arrived safely.

I am blessed to work for family. I have been my uncle's legal secretary for nineteen years (and counting). He was also Daniel's landlord while Daniel lived in Troy. Daniel lived in an apartment on the back side of their house. To say that my "Uncle Boss" was generous, understanding, concerned, and helpful during Daniel's journey is a complete understatement. He gave me all of the time off I needed in order to be with Daniel, help Daniel's parents, and meet with doctors. God knew long ago that this would happen. He knew I would need an incredibly wonderful boss during this time. He provided the perfect people in my life to accommodate the unusual circumstances I would face during this time of my life.

March 1—Troy, Alabama (Facebook Update)
On my way to Atlanta last Friday night I was changing the radio stations. I listen to K-LOVE from Troy to Montgomery, and as far as it will reach Northward. Then I look for JOYFM out of Atlanta to listen to the rest of the drive. As I was changing the stations I ran across a sermon by Adrian Rogers. He was preaching from Genesis 39-41, the story of Joseph. Can you imagine being sold by your own family into slavery, accused of the unthinkable and more, only to come out on top as Prime Minister over the very ones who mistreated you? It's fair to say that there was a time in Joseph's life where he was "at the end of his rope." A comment was made that "if you are at the end of your rope, tie and knot and hold on tight"!

The points made in this sermon that have resonated in my heart are these:
Do not demand to understand.
Do not bow to bitterness.
Do not be unwilling to wait.
Do not fail to be faithful.
Do not let your dreams dissolve.

"Commit your way to the Lord, trust in him and he will do this: He will make your righteous reward shine like the dawn, your vindication like the noonday sun.

**Be still before the Lord and wait patiently for him; do
not fret when people succeed in their way, when they
carry out their wicked schemes. Refrain from anger
and turn from wrath; do not fret – it leads only to evil.
For those who are evil will be destroyed, but those who
hope in the Lord will inherit the land. A little while,
and the wicked will be no more; though you look for
them, they will not be found. But the meek will inherit
the land and enjoy peace and prosperity. The wicked
plot against the righteous and gnash their teeth at
them; but the Lord laughs at the wicked, for he knows
their day is coming." Psalm 37:5–13, NIV**

When Daniel and his parents had scheduled team meetings—meaning
they met with the doctor and therapists in one day—they would ask that
I come for those meetings. At one of the team meetings while Daniel was
still in inpatient rehabilitation, I sat down at a long conference table with
his doctor. I questioned him in detail about Daniel's situation, medications,
things that I could do to help Daniel recover, his prognosis, and so much
more. God really showed out when Dr. Dennison told me that Daniel
was on the absolute minimum medications and minimum dosages for his
condition. That put things in a new perspective for me.

After the meeting was over, I realized I had done all of the talking and
Daniel's parents had not said much. When I asked them if I had talked
too much, they reassured me that I had asked all of their questions, plus
some. I went into that meeting with a written list of questions, ideas, and
suggestions. What can I say? I'm an obsessive-compulsive control freak.

At another team meeting, this time at outpatient therapy, I got to meet
with Dr. Fadia and participate in one-on-one therapy time with Daniel.
Daniel is a quiet person. He always has been. Since I've known him, he
has always been fairly passive and laid back. This didn't always translate
to being a good thing for his doctor and therapists. This particular day,
his doctor questioned me, saying, "How do you think Daniel is doing?" I
told her that I thought he was physically doing great, but I also expressed
my concerns about mild depression, lack of motivation, and medications.
During his therapy sessions that day, I was able to watch Daniel interact

with his therapists. He did everything asked of him, but nothing more. He only spoke when spoken to. That alone didn't concern me because of his quiet, passive nature. But he seemed to be in a fog. That concerned me.

Ritalin. This is not a medication that I wanted Daniel on long-term. We were told that it would help him focus on his therapy. He was also on Amantadine to help him be alert. Strangely enough, one of the side effects of Amantadine is drowsiness. But Amantadine was keeping him high, and Ritalin was bringing him down. In my non-medical mind, these two medications counteracted each other. My thinking was that his sleep cycle had been reset and he was doing well. Why did he need the Amantadine? But the Ritalin is what really concerned me. I firmly believe the Ritalin is what made Daniel seem like he was constantly in another world. I did not attribute that to the brain injury. I felt like it was a result of the medication. I'm not a doctor. I kept my thoughts to myself for a long time. But eventually, I would question the use of these medications long-term.

March 4—Atlanta, Georgia (Facebook Update)

I am so happy and relieved to be in Atlanta with My Daniel! Addison and I are both here and we were 2 happy girls to see him! When we arrived he and his dad were watching basketball. We stayed up and talked a few minutes, then we all got ready for bed.

As I was taking the cushions off the couch, Daniel walked in and reached down and pulled the sofa bed out for me. Now, any normal day in life, I wouldn't have thought twice about it. But without being asked, without any prompting whatsoever (I mean, he could have crawled in his own bed and left me to fend for myself), Daniel came out of the bedroom and back into the living room with the specific purpose of helping me make up the bed for tonight! Awesome mental processing! Not only did Daniel unfold the bed, but he helped me put sheets and a blanket on it! These seem so small and normal until you consider what he has endured and now how far he has come to get where he is now! Thank You, Jesus! The Lord

is hearing our prayers! He is answering! His will for Daniel is perfect! His will for my life is perfect, too! Please keep praying!

Chapter 20

March 5—Atlanta, Georgia (Facebook Update)

OK, Ladies & Gents, Boys & Girls, Prayer Warriors of all ages! My Daniel's surgery has been scheduled for Friday, March 11th! He will have the double cranioplasty done (replacing both bone flaps) at one time. He will remain in Dothan over the weekend and will transfer back to Atlanta on Monday, March 14th! Please be in prayer even now for this surgery. Pray for the neurosurgeon – that he would remain healthy, that his hands would be steady, and that he would see the miracles God has provided so far in Daniel's life (I believe he already acknowledges God in Daniel's life – how could you not?).

Pray for all of the other medical staff who will be taking care of Daniel and assisting in this surgery and recovery. Pray that Daniel and his parents, and those who will be traveling to be with Daniel, will have safe travels! Pray that Daniel will be able to come off of the ventilator easily after the surgery, and there will be no complications during surgery. Pray that Daniel will feel much better after the surgery and that his rehab at Shepherd Pathways will go exceedingly well, blowing the minds of those who work with him! Please continue to pray for the restoration of Daniel's vision. Continue to pray for complete healing of his frontal lobes. Continue to pray for the strength and

determination to get through each new day, and each new task asked of Daniel. PRAY! GOD IS GOOD!

On March 10, 2016, Daniel and his parents traveled from Atlanta back to Dothan. For the first time since being completely unconscious, Daniel would meet the man who saved his life, Dr. Voss. Dr. Voss was completely in awe of the progress Daniel had made in his recovery. He couldn't believe how steady Daniel was on his feet. Daniel communicated well with him. Daniel passed his initial physical exam. He was ready to have his bone flaps replaced.

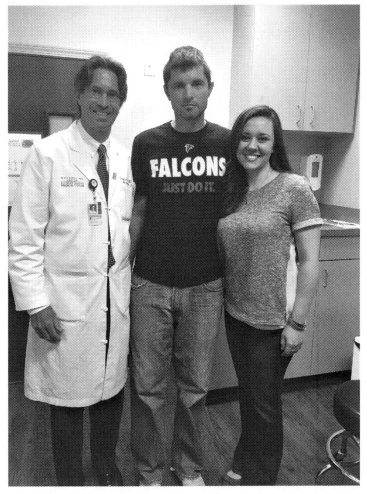

Dr. Voss, Daniel, and Meredith.

The very next day, March 11, we woke up at 4:00 a.m. and started getting things together. I took a few minutes, crawled up in Daniel's lap, and prayed over him. We arrived at the hospital before 6:00 a.m. It wouldn't take very long before Daniel was called back to ready himself for surgery. While we waited for him to be taken for surgery, I called him Humpty Dumpty. But I reminded him that Humpty Dumpty didn't have Dr. Voss and Dr. Hargett to put him back together. He just looked at me and said, "You ain't right." We laughed. That was a big day: the day Humpty Dumpty got put together again.

Daniel and Meredith the morning of surgery.

There is a big God moment in the timing of this surgery. Daniel's surgery was initially tentatively scheduled for late March or early April. God worked it out so that Daniel's surgery would be sooner and he would have the maximum amount of time after the bone flaps were replaced to adjust and recover while still being under the care of the doctors and therapists at Shepherd Center and Shepherd Pathways. God, once again, was in control of the big picture even when we could not see what He was doing.

The surgery took a long time. Daniel's head had to be positioned in a halo to keep it still. To do the first part of the surgery, his head was positioned one way. After that part of the surgery was finished, they had to reposition his head for the other part of the surgery. A drain had to also be placed in the lumbar region of his back in case of excess fluid during surgery. While we waited, we had a room full of prayer warriors. Of course, his parents were there. His brother and sister and their families were there too. My parents also came, as well as his parents' pastor and his wife. The kids and I entertained each other. The vending machine got a lot of attention. But we all waited anxiously for that little buzzer to vibrate and light up with updates on Daniel's surgery.

We finally got the call that all had gone perfectly and Daniel was doing well. His brain was relaxed and without swelling, which meant there was no build-up of excess fluids and the lumbar drain was not needed, and therefore it had already been removed. He would be in recovery for about an hour before being taken to the CCU for at least twenty-four hours. His recovery time turned into much more than an hour while we waited for a room to become available in CCU. But we weren't concerned because we knew he was under the very watchful eye of great nurses. They were kind enough to call us periodically just to let us know he was doing well.

When Daniel was finally taken to CCU, he was a little groggy but awake. We all went back to see him, and he was doing great. His head was bandaged heavily at the top, and bandages were wrapped around his neck and under his chin. All we could see was his handsome face. He had several drains coming from the incision sites, but otherwise he looked wonderfully handsome. He was given a supper tray. He immediately asked that his bed be raised and the tray pulled close. He ate like a champ. Thank you, Lord God.

That night we went back to see Daniel during the last scheduled visitation hour. When we walked in, he was awake but very sleepy. We were standing around talking to him when in came bouncing an energetic, happy nurse. It was our Nurse Brandie! I immediately ran and hugged her tight and thanked God that we had a loving nurse to care for my Daniel that night. It meant so much to have someone familiar with his initial injury to be there to care for him again. Not long after, another familiar face popped in to say hello. Nurse Kris was just down the hall, caring for another patient, when he heard Daniel was back. He too stayed with us for several minutes just catching up on Daniel's progress since he had last seen him. If you remember, Nurse Kris is the Godsend who had previously worked for our neurosurgeons. God continued to line up the perfect care for my Daniel. How awesome is that?

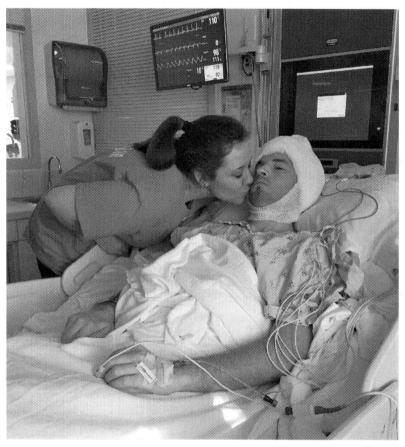

Meredith and Daniel after surgery.

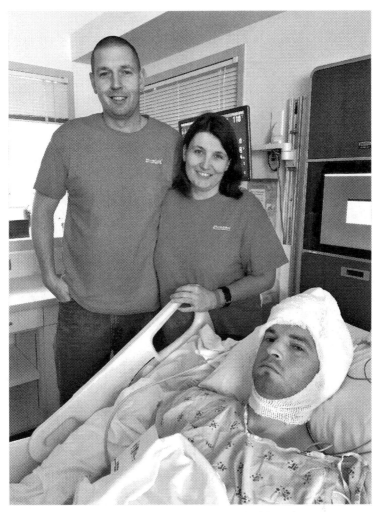

Daniel with his sister, Stephanie, and brother, Ken.

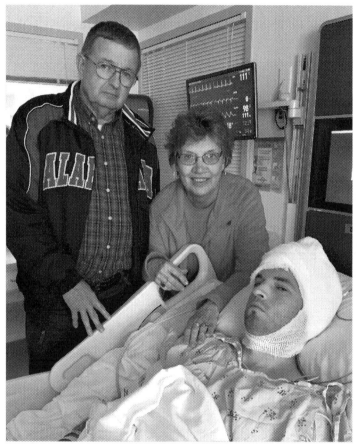

Daniel and his dad, Craig, and mother, Wanda.

Chapter 21

The next day, Daniel was moved from CCU to a room on the neurology floor once again. Just before being moved, he got really sick. The nurses took good care of him and got him cleaned up and comfortable again before moving him. After he was settled in his new room, I sat on the edge of his bed, holding a wet cloth on his face and forehead. I pulled up YouTube on my phone and found a song that had been playing constantly in my mind. "Just Be Held," by Casting Crowns had somewhat been my anthem during this time of trial. I played it and several other songs softly, just trying to ease Daniel's tension.

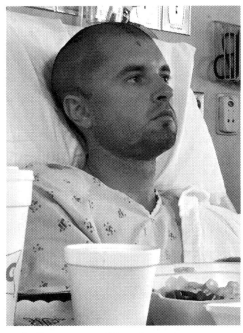

Daniel after surgical bandages were removed.

Not long after that, my parents and daughter arrived at the hospital. Addison was allowed to go into Daniel's room and see him for just a moment, and then my mom took her out into the hallway. I told Daniel I was going to get something to eat with Addison and that I would be back soon. He acknowledged with a slight nod of his head. When I left, his mom came in to sit with him. My parents, Addison, and I ate at Chili's. That is one of Addison's favorite places to eat because of the tabletop games they have for her to play. We enjoyed our dinner and our family time, and then I left to return to the hospital.

On my way back, I stopped at the Sonic across from the hospital and picked up a Sprite for Daniel, and a diet cherry limeade for myself. When I walked into Daniel's room, his parents were both dozing off on the small couch that was in the room. No sooner than I sat my purse and the drinks on the counter, Daniel started gasping and gagging. I grabbed a pan and shoved it in front of him just in time for him to be sick. His parents heard the commotion and woke up to help. I grabbed wet cloths and put them on his head and neck. I felt so helpless. I had never seen Daniel throw up. I hope I never do again.

Daniel would spend that night pretty well medicated and sleeping. I roomed in with Daniel that night so that I could assist him with getting in and out of the bed and helping with whatever he needed. For a while, I stayed up journaling. Daniel was watching television, or so I thought. At one point I looked up and noticed him staring at me. I asked him if he was feeling okay. He told me that he was just tired and ready to go to sleep. I took that as a hint to turn off the lights, and we went to bed.

The next morning, the nurse came in to give Daniel his medications. I wouldn't let him take them until they brought him some crackers or cookies to eat at the same time. We had learned the hard way over the past six weeks that Daniel's stomach doesn't tolerate medications well if it is empty. The nurse kindly obliged and brought some crackers. I'm happy to report that Daniel did not get sick at all that day!

Later in the day, his sister and her family came to visit, as did his brother and his family. You should have seen all twelve of us crammed into that hospital room. I know you won't believe it, but we were actually all well-behaved and quiet so as not to disturb other patients. None of us wanted to be kicked out of Daniel's room for being rowdy, so we were on our best behavior. Daniel's maternal grandparents also made the trip to be with him for surgery and until he returned to Atlanta. My Daniel is loved by so many people. He is truly a blessed man.

Daniel looked much more like himself this day. He was more alert, there was only minimal swelling, and the shape of his head was right again. He was perfect.

That night we had a surprise visitor. Nurse Autumn came by Daniel's room to say hello and check on him. I hugged her and got so emotional. Remember, Nurse Autumn is the nurse in the CCU who caught both of Daniel's neurological changes that caused him to need surgery. She is our angel nurse. Of course, Daniel had no recollection of who she was or what she meant to us, but he would know in time. We would make sure that he knew.

I roomed in with Daniel again that night. That night was one of my favorite nights. Daniel patted his hand on the bed and told me to come sit with him. So I did. We reclined back on his bed, his arm wrapped around me, and watched *The Blind Side* on television. We laughed and joked during the movie and just enjoyed being together. Daniel slept much better that night, which is so important to a patient with a brain injury. God was still certainly at work.

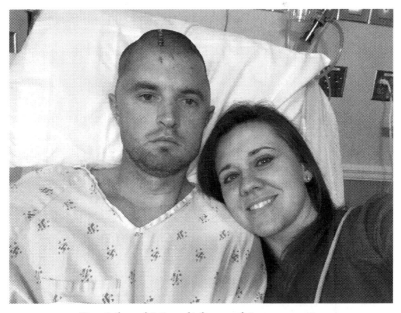

Daniel and Meredith watching a movie.

The next day, Daniel was discharged from the hospital in Dothan. He was wheeled in a wheelchair down to the discharge area. That's when I stopped the nurse and asked him to let Daniel walk out of the hospital. It was a big deal to me to literally have him walk out to the car. In the prayers of so many of our prayer warriors, we asked God to let Daniel walk out of the hospital, and that's exactly what he did. I must admit that Daniel was not happy with me. He was experiencing some discomfort from where the lumbar drain had been placed. However, he did not let that stop him from showing what God had done in his life so far by walking out of that hospital. Standing out beside the car was his supervisor from work. He had come to watch Daniel walk out. They shook hands and spoke briefly, and then Daniel got in the car.

Daniel and his parents drove back to Atlanta. The day after that, Daniel was back in his regular therapy routine. There was significant swelling in his face for almost a week, but after the swelling subsided, he looked perfect. It did take some time for him to adjust to the atmospheric pressure changes now that his bone flaps were back in place, but as God would have it, Daniel's balance adjusted smoothly.

Chapter 22

Daniel had a lot of adjusting to do after his last surgery. Changes were taking place physically and mentally. As I mentioned before, one of the challenges he faced was with pain from where the lumbar drain had been placed during the last surgery. Due to the amount of pain, and the location of the incision, for almost two weeks Daniel walked with a limp, a short gait, almost like he was dragging his left leg. That caused some concern, but thankfully the pain subsided and his gait returned to normal after some time. A lot of the physical adjustments caused confusion for Daniel. He even began experiencing mild depression. Again, I was not going to let him get depressed if I could help it.

**Meredith and Daniel at Shepherd Center.
The light returning to his eyes.**

When Daniel was first admitted to Shepherd Center, I started trying to think outside the box for ways to surprise him. Remember, I brought cupcakes. But I also contacted several sports personalities and players who I thought were in the Atlanta area. I contacted the Atlanta Falcons to see if Julio Jones could visit. I contacted, recently graduated Alabama running back Kenyan Drake's agent to see if he could visit. I contacted Alabama's Coach Nick Saban to see if he would write to Daniel or visit. I didn't hear anything from anyone for two whole months.

I eventually got an e-mail from someone named Julia. Julia was my contact for Kenyan Drake. She was excited to help set up something between Daniel and Kenyan. I gave her some more information about Daniel's current status, e-mailed her a picture of us, and we set a date. April 3, Kenyan Drake would come visit Daniel. I wanted so badly to keep it a secret from Daniel. It was hard, but I did it!

If you followed me on social media, you saw the look on Daniel's face the moment he recognized Kenyan. He was so excited. "What's up, man?" That's how he greeted him. So normal. Kenyan shook hands, hugged necks, signed a picture and a football to Daniel, and sat down with us for more than thirty minutes. One of the most important things Kenyan told

Daniel greeting Kenyan Drake.

Daniel that day was about the scar on his right arm, a result of a broken arm sustained in the game against Mississippi State in 2015, and the surgery to repair the injury. He shared with Daniel that being able to see that scar on a daily basis reminds him that he can still accomplish his dreams, but he has to work that much harder to do so. He was so personable and easy to talk to. His humility blew me away. May he always be humble. I pray this young man goes far in his NFL career and in life.

We ended our visit with a one-on-one interview with an ESPN.com sports writer, Vaughn McClure. He published an article about Daniel and his visit with Kenyan Drake. The article was also shared by www.saturdaydownsouth.com. That will be a day we always remember.

Chapter 23

Do you like to ride roller coasters? I love to ride them at amusement parks. I do not like to ride them in life. One minute you're on a high, the next you've hit bottom. The climb back to the top is slow; then you plummet down again only to be jerked around a sharp corner, leaving you with whiplash like you didn't know existed.

Do you remember that I mentioned Daniel seeing an eye doctor in Atlanta? That eye doctor ordered certain scans to be done to give her a better image of Daniel's optic nerve, pituitary gland, and the occipital region of his brain. In obtaining those images, we also discovered a pretty significant amount of blood in the frontal lobe region of Daniel's brain. What we didn't know was where the blood was coming from: if it was something old that had not absorbed yet or if it was a new problem.

After the images were sent to the neurosurgeon, it was determined that we would wait two weeks and repeat the scans. In the meantime, the eye doctor did several tests to see the limits of Daniel's vision and prescribed glasses with prisms for him to wear. The goal of the prisms was to redirect "true center," both vertically and horizontally, in Daniel's vision. Unfortunately, he couldn't tell much difference.

I won't lie. I got on my knees and had long conversations about Daniel with God. God had brought Daniel way too far to allow for other complications, like a brain bleed, to occur. I know that God's plan is perfect. But I also know He loves hearing from His children. I knew that a long, detailed, heated conversation through prayer would certainly be heard by my Creator who loves me so much. Two weeks later, the scans were repeated. God once again proved His love and faithfulness to His children. The amount of blood had reduced significantly, and it all seemed to be improving. *I hear you. I love you. Keep trusting in me.*

"The More I Seek You" is a song by Kari Jobe, a Christian artist. The beginning lyrics in that song say, "The more I seek you, the more I find you. The more I find you, the more I love you. I wanna sit at your feet, drink from the cup in your hands, lay back against you and breathe, feel your heartbeat." Can you imagine for just a minute? Close your eyes and think about sitting at the feet of Jesus. Imagine there is no one there but you and Jesus. Now read those lyrics once again. Doesn't it make you want to crawl up in the very lap of Jesus and just be still? Imagine the peace that comes at the feet of Jesus. Imagine the comfort.

The Bible tells us, "Come to me, all you who are weary and burdened, and I will give you rest. Take my yoke upon you and learn from me, for I am gentle and humble in heart, and you will find rest for your souls. For my yoke is easy and my burden is light" (Matthew 11:28–30 NIV). Can you hear Jesus whisper those words in your heart? I did. The song I mentioned above was aired on the radio a lot during Daniel's journey. It was usually in the dark of the night when I found myself pouring out my heart to Jesus, trying so desperately to lay my burdens down at His feet and leave them there. Being a fixer, I have a hard time letting go and letting God just work. That has been one of the biggest, most difficult lessons I have had to learn during this journey.

Chapter 24

Daniel's family continued to be tested and tried. Trials seemed to be coming from every direction. One evening after work, I went to our local urgent care facility. I had not been feeling well and hated to ask for time off work during the day to go to the doctor, so I wanted to be seen after hours. While I was sitting in the waiting room that evening, I received a text from Daniel's niece and could tell that something wasn't quite right. I called Daniel's sister to find out what was going on. Daniel's paternal grandmother's house had caught on fire and burned to the ground. Thankfully, someone saw his grandmother and assisted her out of the burning house. However, she lost everything, including her sweet puppy dog.

While that grandmother was being checked out in the local emergency room, Daniel's other grandmother was also being admitted to the hospital with health problems. Both of Daniel's grandmothers were in the hospital. Both of Daniel's parents were almost four hours away with Daniel. I couldn't just sit in Troy and do nothing so I left the urgent care without being seen by the doctor, and drove to Greenville. I knew there wasn't much I could do at the hospital, so I went to the store and bought replacement necessities for the one grandmother who had just lost everything. Then, I went to the hospital to check on our patients. Both were kept overnight for observation, and both were released within a few days. Thankfully, Daniel's bedroom at his parents' house was available for his grandmother to use until she found where she wanted to live more permanently.

Daniel's dad needed to come home and check on his mom and her property loss. I convinced him to come home that Thursday night and assured him that I would drive to Atlanta on Friday night and bring Daniel and his mom home for the weekend. While the weekend was full of uncertainty for the future, it was also a much-needed answer to prayer. Daniel got to return home to Greenville and experience his "normal."

Since Daniel's grandmother was staying in his bedroom at his parents' house, he needed somewhere to sleep. His parents agreed that he could come to Troy with me for the weekend since I had room. That weekend, I watched Daniel fall back into a complete sense of normalcy. He never hesitated with steps in my house. He picked up the television remote and found what he wanted to watch with no problem. He helped himself to the food and drinks in the kitchen. He found the plastic bags under the cabinet that he used to take home his dirty clothes. I watched all of this happen, and I never had to say a word out loud. All the while, I was singing praises of thankfulness in my heart to God.

That Sunday afternoon, I took Daniel back to Greenville. I stayed with him until they had to drive back to Atlanta. As I got ready to leave, Daniel walked me out to my car. This, my friends, was a *God* thing! When Daniel got hurt, I wasn't sure I would ever again walk while holding his hand. I wasn't sure I would hear his voice or experience his sense of humor. I wasn't sure that I would still have a true Southern gentleman. But God allowed me all of these things. He gave my Daniel back to me.

Chapter 25

On May 5, just seven days shy of four months after Daniel's accident, I got off work, emptied my car of all things unnecessary, folded the seats down flat, and drove to Atlanta. I had big plans. That night I would load my car full of groceries, linens, luggage, pictures, posters, and more so that the very next day, I could bring my Daniel home! That next day, May 6, I drove Daniel to Shepherd Pathways. His parents drove over a little while later. Daniel participated in his therapy, and then at lunch, Daniel graduated from the outpatient program at Shepherd Pathways. To God be the Glory! Great things He hath done!

Daniel with his outpatient therapy team at Pathways.

After Daniel's last therapy session in Atlanta, we had one more stop to make. We drove back to Shepherd Center and had the privilege of meeting Mr. James Shepherd, founder of Shepherd Center, and Alabama Crimson Tide Coach Nick Saban. Coach Saban had come to Shepherd Center to meet and encourage the many patients there, especially the fabulous Alabama Crimson Tide fans!

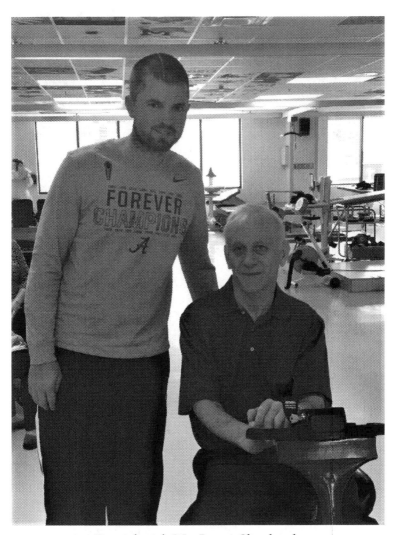

Daniel with Mr. James Shepherd.

**Daniel's dad, Daniel, Coach Nick Saban,
Meredith, and Daniel's mom.**

After meeting Coach Saban, we drove home to Sweet Home Alabama. On the way home, Daniel got hungry, so we stopped at one of his favorite places to eat, Texas Roadhouse, and then continued home. We arrived in Greenville late, so we unloaded the cars and left everything piled on the floor until the next day.

Home. Somewhere Daniel had not been for more than thirty-six hours at a time since Christmas 2015. Remember, Daniel moved to Troy in November 2015, but he did go home to Greenville for Christmas. Being home meant new routines and new schedules. Workers' Compensation case managers worked diligently to find and set up the therapies that Daniel needed to continue after his graduation from Shepherd Center. Speech therapy, physical therapy, and counseling sessions were set up in Montgomery, an hour away from Greenville, two days each week. Due to the location of Greenville and its small-town atmosphere, like many towns in Alabama, it didn't boast a lot of therapeutic opportunities for Daniel. So we had to look outside the box to find what he needed.

After initial evaluations at the new location of his therapy, it was quickly determined that he would not need their physical therapy services for long. He worked diligently with physical therapy for a few months and was released. He continued to work with his speech therapists, and they changed courses to include money management after a while.

A few weeks after graduating from Shepherd Center, Daniel had to return to Atlanta for a complete neuro-psychological exam. The exam would take several hours and would consist of one-on-one time between the psychologist and Daniel, and then also time with Daniel and his parents together. Several weeks later, he had to return to Atlanta for the results of the testing. The results were written out in a nine-page document covering everything from physical appearance to Daniel's money management skills and potential future release for job training and full-time work. He also had a few follow up appointments with his outpatient and inpatient doctors and the eye doctor, while he was there.

I had a list of questions for his inpatient doctor. Unfortunately, I was unable to attend that appointment. Daniel's mother was kind enough to ask my questions and relay the answers back to me. One of my biggest concerns, as I mentioned before, was the long-term use of the medication, Ritalin. The doctor agreed that Daniel could start weaning off of both of his medications. This was such an answer to prayer. Daniel can take Tylenol when needed for headaches, but I am happy to report that today Daniel is on no medication as a result of his injury. Praise God from whom all blessings flow!

On June 16, we returned to the neurosurgeon in Dothan for a follow-up appointment. Again, Dr. Voss was extremely pleased with Daniel's recovery and progress. Daniel talked to him about his desire to go back to work and how well he was feeling. Dr. Voss, Dr. Hargett, and all of the doctors and nurses at Neuro Spine in Dothan were a true blessing and joy in our lives. They were an answer to prayer. We became family. They treated Daniel like a celebrity and loved on him through every step of his recovery.

Dr. Voss was always in tune with what was going on in Atlanta with Daniel's therapy. We could not have asked for better doctors' communications. If you can't see God in that one small aspect of the big picture, then you are blind to the Holy Spirit. How often can you say that your doctors have been only a phone call away and were completely in tune and in communication with other doctors providing your care on a moment's notice? God opened those lines of communication. There is no doubt in my mind. Daniel was released that day to come back in one year for a final follow-up appointment.

Chapter 26

As I sit here and write, my heart is singing, "God is so good. God is so good. God is so good. He's so good to me." I have to tell you a little funny story about that song. When Daniel was in the hospital in Dothan, there was an older lady in the waiting room who was waiting to see her loved one who was also a patient there in CCU. After one of the visitation hours, the lady and I were walking down the hallway together, and she started singing that song. She sang, "God is so good. God is so good. God is so good …" and then out of nowhere, she said, "I need a drink." I never did find out what kind of drink she needed, but I still laugh about that sweet older lady every time I hear that song.

Workers' Compensation and the doctors all worked well together on Daniel's behalf. We are thankful that the best doctors in their fields were approved for Daniel's care. Daniel was accepted as a patient at the Callahan Eye Hospital in Birmingham in their neuro-ophthalmology department. It was our prayer that the doctors there would be able to do something to help Daniel's vision improve. However, that wasn't the case. When Daniel fell, pressure on his brain caused a stroke in the left occipital region of his brain, which caused swelling of his optic nerve. While the optic nerve is still intact, the swelling caused irreversible damage to the nerve.

While at that appointment, mention was made of a possible meningioma on Daniel's brain. A meningioma is a type of brain tumor. I, myself, was diagnosed with a meningioma in 2009, so when the doctor said that word, I immediately saw red flags. The way it was described to me in the past was that a meningioma is a tumor in the tissues around the spinal cord and brain. Thankfully, most of them are benign (non-cancerous); however, they can on rare occasion be malignant (cancerous). Mine was benign and had calcified. Therefore it was not growing. We pray the same results for

Daniel as they watch his meningioma carefully over the coming months and years.

Daniel was discouraged by this news. But he won't let anyone see his disappointment. That's just Daniel. I, on the other hand, had extremely high expectations for this doctor and went home with a heavy heart. When I got to the quiet of my bedroom that night, I fell on my knees and cried out to God with my face buried in the carpet. "Please, God, don't allow this vision deficit to limit Daniel's independence and his ability to drive. Please, God, heal him! The door is wide open for You to do another miracle in Daniel's life, and we will give You all the glory!" With tears in my eyes, I sat up and just stayed there on the floor for a few minutes. We got a lot of news, including some we weren't expecting that day, and I was very emotional.

Even though the results of the appointment in Birmingham were not exactly what we had hoped for, I still did not give up on finding help for Daniel regarding his vision. Since Daniel's injury, two different people, at two different times, have come up to me and mentioned vision therapy. They had experienced great success with their loved ones who had been treated with vision therapy. Both people, independently of each other, mentioned the same specialized practice to me. Coincidence? I think not. I can see God's hand all over it!

I contacted Daniel's Workers' Compensation case manager and asked her what she needed in order for them to be able to pay for vision therapy treatment. She responded right away, and I set out on a mission to get her what she needed. Vision therapy can't hurt, right? It can only help. Daniel's evaluation for vision therapy was set and his treatment plan created. Within the first two weeks of participating in phototherapy, Daniel's fields of vision in both eyes were already responding positively. His visual fields were opening up! Simply staring into a blue/green light for twenty minutes each day, five days each week, had already begun to reset Daniel's nervous system, improve his eyesight, and give Daniel positive results! I have very high expectations because I know that my God is still in control! This is an ongoing process.

Chapter 27

So what does the color pink have to do with any of this? Do you remember throughout this book when I said I was journaling, usually in the middle of the night? I handwrote that journal. It is very long and very detailed about the daily ins and outs of Daniel's care. It tells the good, the bad, and the ugly parts of every single day of his recovery through most of his outpatient rehabilitation days. It even includes pictures that are intermingled with the journaling to correspond with the day they were taken. My journaling started to slow down once Daniel was in outpatient rehab. His days were very much the same, thankfully, because he was doing so well.

Back to the color pink. One Sunday afternoon, I was very emotional after deciding to read the handwritten journal from the start. As I was reading, I would gasp at the recognition of how God answered prayers and how God worked things out in Daniel's favor. I picked up a pink highlighter and started underlining what I called "God Moments" that had been journaled each day. Once I got through the entire journal, I looked back. There sure was *a whole lot of pink!*

God really showed up and showed out for Daniel. What's so special about Daniel? Nothing more than is so special about you! Your very Creator wants to be just as obvious and honored in your life. Our world is so filled with craziness these days that we let God get covered in the dust and rubble of a broken life, rather than rising Him to the top and placing Him on a pedestal in spite of the rubble.

There is absolutely nothing special about me either. I'm just a broken girl, a sinner covered in the blood of Jesus who is not worthy of God's time of day. But because He created me, and because He loves me, He sacrificed everything just so that I could spend eternity with Him in Heaven. But why wait for eternity? I can spend my life on this earth glorifying Him and shouting from the rooftops about His love and goodness! I plan to look for His love in and through my life every single day, from now until eternity. Won't you join me?

"For God so loved the world that He gave his one and only Son, that whoever believes in Him shall not perish but have eternal life" (John 3:16 NIV). That word, *whoever*, includes you. He says to you, *Believe in Me, believe in Jesus, and have the assurance of eternal life in Heaven.* That belief that He is asking of you is called faith. *Faith* is believing in something you cannot see. Imagine the wind. You cannot see the wind, but you can see the effects of the wind in the moving trees and falling leaves, even feel it in the coolness of a breeze. We cannot see Jesus, yet. But we can most definitely see and feel his power through the Holy Spirit who comes to live in our hearts when we have faith in Him.

You don't have to know the Bible inside and out. You simply have to recognize the sin in your life and the need for God's forgiveness. You have to have faith that Jesus is who He said He is and believe that He died a cruel death on a cross to cover and pay for your sin. You have to believe that He rose from the dead three days later to conquer death so that we can live eternally with Him. Then be willing to repent of, to turn away from, the sin in your life and seek Christ's will for you instead. If you can believe those things, you can commit your heart to Jesus Christ and experience a freedom from eternity separated from Him.

You can learn more about many things in the Bible as you grow as a Christian. Just come with a willing heart to accept Jesus as your Savior. Get yourself into a Bible teaching church where you can be fed spiritually and nurtured into a more mature Christian. And love Jesus. Just love Him and look for Him in every aspect of your life. He is there. Trust me. He is waiting to show out in your life just like He has in Daniel's life, with a whole lot of pink.

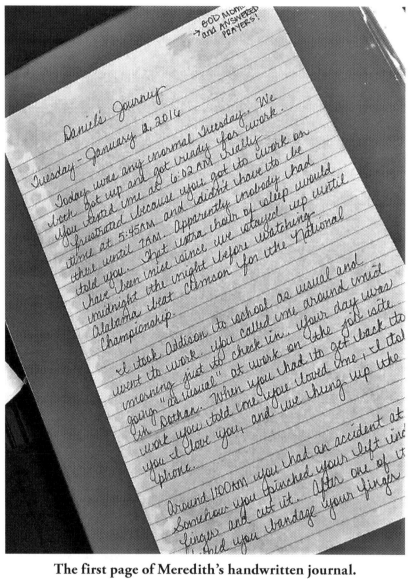

The first page of Meredith's handwritten journal.

Epilogue

This book may have ended, but the healing process for Daniel continues. Daniel has now been released from his neurosurgeon's care. To God be the glory! We continue to covet your prayers and hope that you will join in our celebrations of healing with us as Daniel faces each new day. The Lord has not failed us so far, and we know He will continue to work miracles in Daniel's life. I am so thankful that I get to have a front-row seat to see them firsthand.

Our prayer warriors have been our lifeline. If you can surround yourself with praying individuals, near and far, then do so. You will find that you gain great strength from their willingness to pray. And love Jesus. We do! May God bless you richly!

Love in Christ,
Meredith

Daniel, Meredith, and Addison 14 months after Daniel's accident.

Printed in the United States
By Bookmasters